What do successful people say about D

negotiation skills and his unique abilit}
advise clients?

"This book is an exceptional way to learn the finer points of negotiation and to improve your results"

— Jeremy Wilson, Chairman, Bloomsbury Publishing PLC
and Vice Chairman Barclays Corporate, Barclays Bank PLC

"In this book you will find everything you need to know about negotiating from the largest deal to negotiating where to go on holiday with your partner. Absorb it and watch your results, relationships and rewards improve dramatically"

— Dr Nido Qubein, International best selling author, President High Point
University, North Carolina, Mentor and Coach

"I have worked with Derek for over 20 years as a competitor and customer (of his training business): he is able to translate theory into practice in a way that makes people think differently about a situation or challenge creating powerful outcomes."

— Steve Pateman, Head of UK Corporate
and Commercial Banking, Santander Bank UK plc

"Derek's negotiation advice has been invaluable to me in both my business dealings and as I travel the world in my duties as President of the Global Speakers Federation. In this book you will learn all you need to know about negotiating."

— Alan Stevens, President of the Global Speakers Federation
and 'The Media Coach'

"Derek has incorporated the gems of his excellent material, on this important topic, into this book. It is a must for negotiators whatever their levels of experience: a handy refresher for hardened professionals and a useful and comprehensive handbook for those new to the challenges."

— Michael Williams, Chairman Sovereign Business Systems

"Derek Arden is a power negotiator. This book is written for negotiating at all levels of corporate and social life. It is packed with great insights and tips."
— Julie Garland-McLellon, Professional Non-Executive Director

"This book is a must for anyone who negotiates. Derek has given me so much advice on how to negotiate great discounts and win win resolutions in my business. His negotiation articles for my magazine and websites are always the most read and most popular. He is THE expert on negotiation."

— Matthew Tumbridge, Managing Director, Used Car Expert

"This book is the definitive answer to negotiating business and personal relationships, easy to read and understand, a must have."

— Godfrey Lancashire, Managing Director, London House International Limited

"Derek's drive, energy and negotiation skills have helped us secure savings of over £200,000 per year reducing our total payments for these services by over 50%. We have asked Derek to continue to be our Strategic Negotiation Advisor on key issues and are delighted he has agreed to do so."

— John Shaw – Finance and IT Director, Oxfam

"Derek has been working with me for the past three years as a mentor and a coach. This has enabled me to focus beyond education and see how the business world would handle similar issues. Derek has introduced business models which have helped our teams understand the very challenging and competitive world as we educate the next generation of leaders."

— Sue Bullen, Headteacher, Woolmer Hill School

"Thank you so much for your educational keynote. You grabbed the room, challenged them, and gave huge value in return for their attention! "

— Kenny Harris, President, Professional Speaking Association, Scotland

POWER NEGOTIATING

HOW TO NEGOTIATE ANYTHING, ANYTIME, ANYWHERE

DEREK ARDEN

Tiptree House

TH First published in Great Britain by Tiptree House Publishing 2011

Copyright ©Derek Arden International Limited and Tiptree House Publishing

Design and layout by Ayd Instone, www.sunmakers.co.uk

ISBN: 978-0-9559568-1-2

Version 1.2

To Sally, Mark and Jenny

Thanks for all your love, support and understanding.

Also by Derek Arden

Books

Presenting Phenomenally – How to present confidently, clearly and charismatically

The Secrets of How to Negotiate your Salary

Pocket Guides

117 Handy Haggling Hints – how to negotiate win win win deals

Body Language - The Secret Language of Success

Workbooks

Advanced Negotiation Skills

Street Savvy – Sales, Influencing and Negotiation success

Audio CD's – MP3

Negotiate success – live at Surrey University Business School.

The 97 tips that the top negotiators don't want you to know.

Executive briefings

Monthly action packed briefings, tips and techniques.

To sign up go to www.DerekArden.com

For more infomation, contact: action@derekarden.co.uk

www.derekarden.com

www.derekarden.co.uk/blog

www.youtube/derekarden

DISCLAIMER

Negotiation skills are not a quick fix. Anyone who decides to become a competent negotiator must expect to invest a lot of time and effort in improving their skills.

The purpose of this book is to educate based on the author's experience as well as selected information available up to the printing date.

It is not the purpose of this book to reprint all the information that is otherwise available to negotiators, business people and individuals but to complement, amplify and supplement such other information.

Every effort has been made to make this book as complete as possible. However, as the book is intended and construed as a general guide only, it should not be perceived as, and is not intended to be, the ultimate source of negotiation or negotiating.

The book provides information about the subject matter covered. Neither the author, nor the publisher, render legal, accounting or other professional advice or services and the book should not be read or understood as such. The author and the publisher hereby disclaim all and any responsibility and liability caused or alleged to be caused directly or indirectly by the information contained in this book.

Should you wish or need any legal or other expert assistance, you are required to consult with a competent professional advisor.

Contents

Contents

Section 3: Tactics and Strategies

Section 4: Unlocking the Power

Foreword
By Sir Gerry Robinson

I first met Derek Arden many years ago when I was Chief Executive of the Granada Group, I was negotiating the financing of the £3 billion hostile takeover of the Forte Hotel chain.

We had been badly let down by one large financial institution when they changed their mind to help, at the last minute. Derek and his team stepped in and negotiated into the late hours, over a weekend, to increase the amount Barclays and the other banks would underwrite.

The pricing was high and higher than we wanted to pay. To keep the ongoing relationship in balance and the deal in place Derek and the team worked tirelessly to re-negotiate the shape of the deal to help us and keep the consortium of banks in place.

Derek's clear thinking enabled us to negotiate a win win transaction.

My philosophy has been - Keep your negotiations simple and focused.

In this book you will learn everything you need to learn to negotiate anything, anytime and anywhere.

Enjoy and learn from Derek.

Sir Gerry Robinson

Introduction

There are aggressive hardball negotiations, that's how wars happen.

There are uncompromising union negotiations, that's how some union representatives keep their jobs.

There are some advisers who encourage their clients to sue for every penny they can get, that's how they get rich.

Negotiation does not have to be confrontational. It can and should be collaborative. **You get what you want and we get what we want. Win Win.**

There is a third win, now we have built a relationship and trust, we can do business together in the future, perhaps for many years. That's Win Win Win.

Negotiation take place 24/7 - whether it's deciding with your partner where you are going on holiday, to which restaurant you might go, who is going to pick up the children or what time to return from the football match.

This book covers all areas of negotiations, including the more advanced negotiation issues that you may experience in business.

Some of the best negotiations take place unknowingly, but so do some of the least beneficial.

Whatever the situation, this book will make you a winner.

The bargaining and haggling process often follows a pattern. This book will help you be aware of strategies and tactics others are using and how to use them yourself.

As you do all this your confidence will rise, and your results will improve.

- If you are an experienced negotiator with many years of experience dealing with difficult situations, you may like to go straight to section 3, before you read the rest of the book.

- If you are relatively new to negotiating, start the book at the front making notes, in the notes section at the back of each chapter.

Good luck in all your negotiations.

Derek Arden
Guildford, Surrey, UK

Power Negotiating

Negotiation is a key part of day to day life.

There are many definitions of negotiation.

Here are three I like -

1. Negotiation is any discussion to get a mutual agreement between two or more people.

2. Negotiation is about reaching agreement with other parties so that you can achieve your goals.

3. Negotiation involves an element of trade or bargaining – an exchange of a valuable resource for another, to enable both parties to achieve a satisfactory outcome.

Often people fail to realise that interactions during the day are a form of negotiation.

You will see later in the book there is always the opportunity to negotiate, whenever you want something. Even when you don't think it is possible.

Think about considering the mindset "Anything and everything is negotiable" and every interaction with another person or another business is a negotiation.

Think of the word negotiation as a chance of three levels of success:

1. To improve your income.

2. To reduce your costs.

3. To improve your relationships.

Now it might seem that this is not possible. Not true. In many cases it will be difficult to achieve all three at the same time, however not impossible if you change your mindset towards negotiation.

In the late 1980s the Harvard Negotiating Project was set up to see how confrontation between countries, religions and tribal situations could be better handled. Finding out what the issues were and how they could be better met.

The seriousness of the conflicts we see around the world now and how they could escalate show why win win win negotiating has to be the way forward.

When you are negotiating consider all the positions. Where you are, where they are and what do we both really want to achieve?

Consider your best position, your target position and your walk away position; then imagine how they see their positions.

Ask questions, listen to the answers carefully and search for the real meanings.

Beware of strategies and tactics and remember that often they work below the level of immediate conscious awareness.

If you are going to a meeting or discussing key issues on the phone, have someone with you.

The bargaining / haggling process often follows a pattern. Look for unreasonable offers, things that need checking out and making sure the outcome is going to be win win win, if that is possible.

Price is important, but as long as you are being realistic, the real issues are usually service, quality, delivery, extras, the relationship, the new ideas etc. Look at your variables. The small inexpensive items that you can include or upsell to close the deal. Think outside the box to find mutual solutions to issues. As you do all this your confidence will rise, and your results will improve. As you read on you will find tips and techniques to help you with all this and other issues in all of your negotiations.

When we position ourselves in a negotiation, perception of power depends on how we see ourselves and how the other party sees themselves.

However we need to research thoroughly both positions so we can really understand the issues. Then we make good decisions. Long term, lasting and quality decisions.

When Winston Churchill became Prime Minister of the United Kingdom on the 10th May 1940, it was perceived that Britain was on its knees, unprepared for war. Germany was strong and moving into countries like Poland, Holland, Norway and about to invade France. Many of the members of parliament in the cabinet wanted a compromise solution with Hitler. They were suggesting trading some colonies for the promise that Britain would be left alone. Churchill despite understanding the weakness of the position the UK faced also understood that negotiating with Hitler was not an option, on the basis of his previous promises to others. Britain was not in a powerful position but would have been in a less powerful position in a few months time if it had compromised its position at that point. Churchill met individually and secretly with many cabinet members persuading them that compromise with someone like Hitler was not an option.

At that point in time the leaders of the UK saw where the country was and started increasing its power with information, with proper resourcing and with a motivational leader who had looked at all the options

Assessing positions, assessing where the power is and how you can increase your power to ultimately negotiate a win win win with sensibly rational people is the purpose of this book.

A final thought before you start this book:

In a conflict there are often three views, mine, yours and the right one. Engaging in a negotiation or a dispute before you think about this carefully is not a good idea. Take a time out before you act.

"Let us never negotiate out of fear, but let us never fear to negotiate"

— John F. Kennedy

Section 1:

Fundamentals
of Power Negotiating

- **Negotiating with yourself**

- **The cost of failure to negotiate**

- **The WIN WIN WIN of negotiating**

- **Who has the power?**

1

Negotiating with yourself

Develop a mindset to always negotiate.

If you always do, what you have always done, you will always get what you have always got.

I am always amazed when I speak at conferences on negotiating. I look at the audience and ask a very simple question.

"How many of you are negotiators?"

I get very few hands up. I get just a few nods.

Of course the real answer is that we are all negotiators. We negotiate all the time.

Negotiation is a 24 / 7 / 365 skill

Every human interaction is a negotiation and we learn to be good at it early on as a child. In fact almost as soon as we are born, we cry and find that crying gets us fed.

If you asked a behavioural psychologist what that does to us, they would say that the response becomes an anchor. "A Pavlovian response". Make a fuss and you get attention.

Of course as we grow up we learn that there are better ways of getting what we want.

Dale Carnegie wrote one of the first and still one of the best interpersonal skills books over 70 years ago, with the great title, 'How to win friends and influence people.'

It has been reprinted many times. In essence it says:

If you help people get what they want, they will help you get what you want.

Ages of negotiators

Research has shown that the best ages for negotiating are 0 -16 and 32 to 50.

Up to 16, we are pretty uninhibited. Before our teens we push the boundaries of discovery. In our teens we can be pretty awkward, as we prepare to leave the nest and find out as much as we can about life. So in those years we are pretty much in it for ourselves, pushing our luck as much as we can.

Around 16 we become more aware of what is going on around us, and stop asking. Asking is one of the most important skills in negotiating. Asking great questions and listening carefully. With the stopping of asking as we mature, and as we respect other people more, comes the embarrassment of asking in negotiation scenarios.

Then at about 32, people who are moderately to seriously ambitious, start taking more serious responsibilities in business and realise that they have to go for it. They get stuck in, negotiate and show what they can do.

Around 50, they ease off as they might prefer quicker deals, with less emphasis on the smaller detail.

Life is a choice

It is our life and we can choose whether to get the maximum out of it or not.

There are always choices, although some people prefer not to give it much thought and just hope for the best.

I remember a friend of mine called Mike who said "I am stuck in a job going nowhere, a job with no prospects and I have a large mortgage".

Mike had a choice. He could continue to do nothing and feel sorry for himself or decide to take action and sort himself and his life out.

The vast majority of people decide to take the passive route of doing nothing and wonder why it is nothing that they end up with.

Take action, start negotiating.

The 1st Negotiation is with you and this is in your mind.

"The journey of a thousand miles starts with the 1st footstep"

— Chinese proverb

In Mike's case he had to give up certain things in order to gain others. Whilst we live in an abundant universe there are some things which are finite.

The main finite thing we all have is the amount of time we have.

We all have the same amount of hours in a day, minutes in an hour and seconds in a minute.

It is about energy management. Managing your energy and your motivation. Motivation is helped by setting yourself targets.

There are 24 hours in a day during which the average person sleeps for 7.5 hours, travels for 2 hours, eats for 1.5 hours and works for 8 hours. This leaves 5 hours spare for other interests, which is a massive 35 hours a week.

You have lots of time to take forward your life in a different direction.

So Mike sat down and thought about where he wanted to be in all aspects of his life. He then imagined he had done it, 8 years down the track.

He visualised what he looked like, how he felt, what sounds he was hearing in his head and how people perceived him. He felt good.

Having drawn up his plan, he started taking action. His life changed, he started negotiating with himself and with others and he is now very successful.

You are the most important person in the world. Until you look after you, you cannot help others. That is why when you get on an aeroplane they tell you to put your own oxygen mask on first before you help others.

Another question I ask audiences on my business master-classes is:

"Who do you work for?"

Of course the answer is you work for yourself. You might get paid and rewarded by someone else, a company or a business, but you are selling your time and your skills to someone else in exchange for payment.

Why not look at it as if you work for ME plc. That is your company. Who are your shareholders, who are your stakeholders, who are the people you look after?

Generally, people get paid fairly as the law of supply and demand dictates. However there are always exceptions. Make sure you are not an exception, unless it is in your favour!

The idea to write the book 'The Secrets of How to Negotiate your Salary' was written specifically after three people asked my advice on how to increase their pay, their wages and their salary.

WII FM

The WII FM is always a great thought to have in your mind.

WII FM stands for 'What's In It For Me'

Who is the most important person in the world?

Well despite what we might say publicly, it is you.

This of course works for everyone in the world.

Therefore if you want to get your way, help the other person get their way.

Power Tips

- Take action. Action is the key that unlocks opportunity.

- If you are concerned that the other person might say NO, remember they might say yes.

- Remember WII FM. What's in it for me.

- The first negotiation is with yourself. Make sure you have the mindset "Everything and anything is negotiable"

1.1 Notes

1.1 Notes

....
....
....
....
....
....
....
....
....
....
....
....
....
....
....
....
....
....
....
....
....

2
The cost of failing to negotiate

Use your own negotiation analysis scoresheet.

Work out your negotiating IQ.

As an introduction to this chapter I want to alert you to some numbers.

The cost of not negotiating is expensive!

I have calculated that since I started negotiating seriously over 20 years ago, I may have made or saved over £250,000 after I take into account compound interest.

If you saved just 10% of that over the next 20 years of your life then you would save £25,000 and some of this would be tax free as it is money that you have already paid tax on.

Overleaf is a worksheet which I call the negotiation savings calculator. Get your pen out and do a quick calculation on how much you might make or save over the next 20 years if you negotiate seriously on everything.

You may be surprised how much extra money you might make.

If you are employed, income will be increased pay, salary, bonuses together with extras such as extra allowances, pension contributions and training days etc.

If you work for yourself, income will be increased fees, prices and product sales.

Costs are costs. We should reduce our costs as much as we can. Shop around, price match, ask, ask, ask for lower prices -

1. If you don't ask you don't get.

2. If you don't ask you don't give the other person the opportunity to say yes.

3. 'If you don't ask, the answer is no'. One of my clients told me this is what she tells her three children.

You will see on the *Negotiation Savings Calculator* I have included a third category called "soft pound" deals or bartering.

It is amazing how much you can save by using your skills to help others and they use their skills to help you, without any money changing hands.

Someone might fix my computer and I might give them some coaching on how to raise their fees.

Negotiation Savings Calculator

Sales – Income

Increase by Negotiation   =

Purchases – Costs

Decrease by Negotiation   =

Barter, soft pound deals – deals

Value increase by Negotiation   =

Total extra value – per annum   =

Total extra value per year, multiplied by number of years savings, multiplied by compound investment rate over last period. (over the last 100 year period the average return on stocks and shares and property investments have been over 12% pa)

Exactly the same calculation can be done for your business negotiations.

Earnings and Negotiation skills

I was privileged to be a visiting lecturer for over 12 years, at the Henley Management College, whilst I was working for the Barclays Group. Here they kept records, over a two year period, of the people who attended the Strategic Management Course.

The course was for delegates, in senior management positions, from all over the world, who had been chosen to attend by their company, because of their high potential.

The records related to how their line managers and peers rated certain skills. This was then compared with how much they earned. The typical manager attending was responsible for an average of 231 people.

What the research showed was that a small number of delegates 11%, whose salary was double that of the average attendee, were rated by their manager as strongest in these 5 competences, out of a total of 40 competences:

- Negotiating skills
- Presentation skills
- Oral expression
- Appraisal of subordinates
- Self – management

One of the benefits of using this book to increase your skills is that you are increasing your skills in one of the most important and effective subjects.

High achievers know how to get things done through people. They know how to get things from other people and they know how to make other people feel good.

I was speaking at a conference in Dunfermline, Scotland. A lady in the audience was giving me a particularly evil eye. Her body language was saying there is no way I am going to negotiate. Afterwards I asked her why she was giving me such negative vibes. She said that she felt negotiating price was particularly demeaning and people should always offer their best price, therefore negotiating should not be necessary.

I didn't know what to say, she clearly didn't understand business and how things worked in the world. Sometimes I say to people, negotiate to help the other side stay honest. Help them keep their prices realistic. To this lady it was degrading to negotiate, she would rather pay the list price.

Personal Assessment Scoresheet

Try this self-assessment negotiation questionnaire to help you and your team assess your skills.

First, recall a recent negotiation. Score yourself on your skills and ability in that negotiation and give yourself a score out of 5 on the grid where 5 = high and 1 = low.

If you want to improve your all round skills and negotiation results you need to work individually on these techniques, which directly affect the negotiation result.

Then multiply your scores by the weightings and add up the total to discover how good you are at negotiating.

We can all improve. The difference that makes the difference to the success of your negotiations may be a very small thing which may make a big difference to the result.

Score yourself again after using this book (see chapter 4.3) and then again in three months time. At that time re-read the notes and consider, how you can help your colleagues, friends and family in improving their negotiating skills.

Personal Assessment Scoresheet: Your negotiation IQ

(5 = high, 1 = low)

Preparation: .... x5 = ...

Questioning: .... x1 = ...

Listening Skills: .... x2 = ...

Interpreting Body Language: .... x1 = ...

Managing your own Body Language: .... x1 = ...

Empathy: .... x2 = ...

Understanding Negotiating Tactics: .... x2 = ...

Bargaining skills: .... x3 = ...

Inventing solutions: .... x2 = ...

Confidence: .... x1 = ...

Total: ....

What skills do you need to work on? Rescore yourself in 3 months time after you have practiced some of these skills.

Good all round negotiators should be scoring well over 80.

Power Tips

- Negotiate to have more wealth.

- Negotiate to get a better job.

- If you don't negotiate someone else will get the benefits that you might get.

- Keep checking yourself and improving your scores on the Personal Assessment Scoresheet on p34.

2. Notes

....
....
....
....
....
....
....
....
....
....
....
....
....
....
....
....
....
....
....
....
....
....
....
....

3
The WIN WIN WIN
of negotiating

Some people like negotiating and others don't.

Negotiating is all about being brave, being a little competitive and getting better deals.

I have travelled and spoken extensively all over the world and the following two facts are interesting:

There are two types of people in the world:

1. People who do negotiate.

2. People who don't negotiate.

There are two prices in the world

1. For people who do negotiate.

2. For people who don't negotiate.

How much people negotiate varies all over the world and in different cultures.

Types of Negotiation

Negotiation is central to everything we do in life.

When we have a discussion with someone and something is decided, that is the basic premise of any negotiation

So therefore the spin off from this is to make sure the negotiation starts well and ends well for a WIN WIN WIN.

The word negotiation covers every aspect of interaction in interpersonal skills.

Below I have listed the ING's of negotiating so that we can apply the principles whenever we are in these modes.

The INGs of negotiating

Selling	Influencing	Persuading
Questioning	Listening	Haggling
Bargaining	Trading	Cajoling
Manoeuvring	Manipulating	Bullying
Harassing	Encouraging	Partnership handling

Win / Win / Win negotiation can be the only way forward in this competitive and increasingly globally challenging and dangerous world.

Let's look at the game of two board noughts and crosses, as an introduction to win win win scenarios. Two people play.

Instructions

The game is exactly the same as normal noughts and crosses, and in some countries it is called tic-tac-toe. However there are two exceptions,

1. You can play both boards at the same time.

2. You cannot speak to the person you are playing with.

The objectives of the game are to score as many winning lines as possible. Find a partner and play before turning over this page.

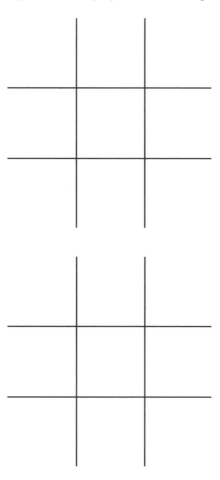

Did you remember the objective was to score as many winning lines as possible? If you co-operate with your partner then there are 8 winning lines each:

X	X	X
X	X	X
X	X	X

0	0	0
0	0	0
0	0	0

However what happens in 91% of the situations (and I have played this game with over 11,000 delegates, across 20 countries and 4 continents) is that human competitiveness is switched on by the mere assumption that the objective is to get more for me and less for you to win.

To get 8 winning lines each, my crosses go on the top board and your noughts go on the bottom board thereby achieving as much for me, and as much for you, by co-operation. A real win win win.

Win, Win, Win – the fifth dimension

Many would say there are 4 outcomes to a negotiation:-

- WIN/WIN
- WIN/LOSE
- LOSE/WIN
- LOSE/LOSE

There is a fifth option - Win, Win, Win.

- A WIN for you
- A WIN for me
- A WIN for us *and* our ongoing relationship

There is a sixth element which is just WIN. The person you are negotiating with does not care what happens to you as long as they win. *Be careful with this person.*

If you chart these strategies graphically you can see the outcome. The vertical axis is the deal or the transaction and the horizontal axis is the ongoing relationship:

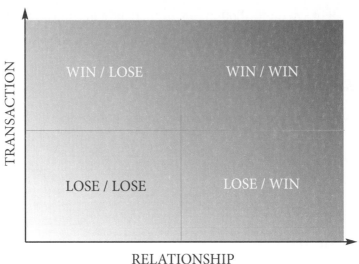

The negotiating strategy you adopt should be directly linked to your business strategy with each individual customer.

This will enable you to maximise your profit either on a long or short-term basis.

Make sure your people know what your strategy is and act accordingly.

In a long-term partnership the synergistic benefits of a truly Win, Win, Win situation cannot be overestimated.

Never forget that it is vital that all members of your team understand your strategy. If they don't, you risk not achieving your goals.

One of the exercises I saw at the Harvard Business School was the push back exercise.

This was demonstrated by Professor William Ury who wrote the ground breaking book "Getting to Yes", which first discussed the issues of win win negotiation.

He asked one of the members of the seminar to come up and centre themselves (both feet planted firmly on the ground the weight distributed evenly) with their palms out stretched.

He took the opposite position. You could try it with a partner.

As he leant and pushed against the person, the person pushed back, in a competitive manner. The harder he pushed the harder the other person pushed to maintain balance and not be pushed over.

How hard are you pushing? Sometimes you should stand aside and re-assess the situation? Letting the right side of the brain think about the big picture and come up with alternatives.

This often happens in life, the harder someone pushes; the harder the other side pushes back, perhaps to the detriment of the situation, the outcome, the deal.

Then Professor Ury did a strange thing. He stopped pushing and moved to the side. The delegate had nothing to push against.

The energy was not there.

Sometimes we have to move to the side and stop pushing to see the big picture.

There is an old parable that goes back many thousands of years.

An old man dies leaving 3 sons. His will is to give one half of his possessions to his eldest, one third to his second born and one ninth to his youngest.

Now at the time of his death he had 17 camels and no other possessions.

The sons couldn't figure out how to do this as the maths wouldn't work. A wise old woman came by and asked if she could help.

They told her the dilemma. She said maybe she could help by offering to give them one of her camels, as a gift.

This would mean that they had 18 camels

> *Half = 9*
>
> *Third = 6*
>
> *Ninth = 2*

Problem solved

However the sons found that they had one camel left, so they gave the camel back to the wise old woman and they all went on their way.

There is more than just one way to resolve a situation.

Look for a win / win / win.

Power Tips

- Look for a win win win strategy when you negotiate.

- Remember the two board noughts and crosses scenario. Everybody wins.

- Stand aside to reassess a situation.

3. Notes

3. Notes

....
....
....
....
....
....
....
....
....
....
....
....
....
....
....
....
....
....
....
....
....

4
Who has the power?

The person with the money generally has the power.

A fool and his money are soon parted.

Power is a key issue when negotiating

Power is important. However, people without power can often create some.

There is a psychological defence mechanism built into a large majority of people to focus on their weaknesses rather than their strengths.

A can't do culture rather than a can do culture.

This can have real consequences in negotiating. If you are one of those people, you might assume that you are in a weaker position than you are and will not ask, for fear of being rejected. This is crazy. If the majority are doing this then no wonder it is easy for the more sophisticated negotiator to get a good deal.

Just look at the business television programmes which are appearing all over the world. They are called *Dragons Den* or something similar. The novice entrepreneur goes in and presents their idea and they get taken for the softest deal, which the rich business people can negotiate. Yes it is venture capital, yes they are business angels and yes this type of money comes at a price but let's look at the scenario.

The only business ideas that get accepted are really good. The synergies are good and the rich business people know they are onto a winner. Yet they want a larger slice of the action than they might get, because they have the power, the prestige and the money.

Occasionally you see someone stand up to them. Good for them.

You have to think through the situation. Talk to people. Take advice but don't pay heavily for it. Be careful who you seek advice from. Make sure they are real experts.

Remember WIIFM – What's in it for me

The issue with some professional advisors is that they often take no risk and charge you for the advice.

Remember always get advice from someone experienced who has been there and done it.

Power can be a perception

Good negotiators will always want the other side to feel they are in a weaker position. That is their game plan.

When you are negotiating you have to let the other side know that you have options. You may have to create options. Tactics, which are covered in chapter 12, are used to make the other side think they are in a weaker position than they really are.

"You can't choose the cards you are dealt but you can make sure you play them in the best way"

— Alvin Law

Always remember to create three options.

There are always three options. The one you want, a softer option and a wild card option. If you don't have three options, create them.

Brainstorm the options that you have. Think outside the box.

Consider the options the other party in the negotiation has, where they are coming from, what they want and how they might play their cards? Check and re check .

Try this exercise. Join the nine dots up with four straight lines without taking your pen off the paper.

·　　·　　·

·　　·　　·

·　　·　　·

Try it before reading on. If you ASSume that this is a box, you cannot do it. You have to take your pen twice outside the box to solve the problem.

> If you assume the other side has the power then they will have. If you look outside the box and think outside the box you might discover what other options are available to you. There are always options, it's just finding them.

Remember there are always options. It is a great idea when you are negotiating to list three options that you have on a piece of paper. Then consider how you can develop these options to increase your power.

In the movie Pretty Woman there is a scene when Richard Gere is lost and is looking for the Beverley Wilshire hotel. He stops his car and asks Julia Roberts for directions. Julia Roberts says that will be five dollars for directions. He says you can't charge me for directions and she says, "I have the information and you want it – it's TEN dollars now because I am busy".

He is in a hurry and she has the information. She has the power and she got paid.

Success is predictable if you do just one thing -

DO what successful people do

"A man often has two reasons for the things he does
– a good one and the real one"

— J. P. Morgan

Power Tips

- Options create power. Make sure you have three options.

- Law of Requisite Variety says the person with the most options gets the best results.

- Power is a perception both in your mind and in the mind of the other side.

The solution to the 9 dots puzzle:

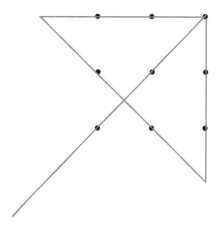

Often the solution is outside the box.

4. Notes

....
....
....
....
....
....
....
....
....
....
....
....
....
....
....
....
....
....
....
....
....
....

4. Notes

Section 2:

Key Secrets
to become a Power Negotiator

- **Prepare, plan and perform**

- **First impressions in negotiating**

- **Asking the right questions**

- **Listening**

- **Sensory awareness**

- **Reading body language**

- **The truth about lying**

5
Prepare, plan and perform

Proper Preparation Prevents Pretty Poor Performance

Prepare – prepare - prepare

Fail to prepare – prepare to fail

"The more I practice the luckier I get." — Gary Player

Preparation is the key that creates a successful negotiation.

Preparation comes in all sorts of formats. However there is no substitute for getting all the facts and considering how you might play your hand.

At the same time look at all the facts of the other side, as best you possibly can and consider how they might play their hand.

Many people are lazy. On a workshop a little while ago I was asked "Is there any way I can avoid spending so much time preparing for an important negotiation?"

I gave the delegate the 'magic' answer, which she didn't want to hear. There is no way you can avoid preparing in full, the 'magic' is in the preparation.

"Opportunity is the haughty goddess that wastes no time on those who are unprepared"

— From the fable *"The Richest Man in Babylon"*

Let's systemise the preparation stage

- What are our goals?

- What do we want to achieve?

- What is the outcome we want for both sides?

- Make sure we brainstorm all the issues.

If we know how the other side has negotiated before, we need to assess it. People usually behave in the same way.

- Do they start high and come down?

- Do they play hardball?

- Do they tell the truth?

- Do they expect our 1st offer to be the real one?

- Do they play games?

- How do they use tactics?

- Do they come down in small amounts?

- Have they got a time issue?

- Have they got a financial issue?

- Is there a new model coming out soon?

- Is their kit a little obsolete?

- What is the service record?

- Do they believe in win win win?

- Does their track record stand up to scrutiny?

- Are they ethical?

- Are they environmentally sound?

- What negotiable variables do they have?

- What negotiable variables do we have?

- Should we use ploys?

- Can we soften them up?

- Do we have enough *what ifs*?

- Should we role play this in real time?

- Might we record it and play it back?

- Who do we know that we can speak to, to find out more about where they are coming from?

- Have we really researched this properly?

- Are there any cultural issues we haven't thought about?

- Do we need a team?

- What will the team role be?

- Where is the power?

2

Key Secrets

Remember the iceberg principle: 90% of the issues are not always apparent, they are below the surface

Positions

As part of our preparation we must consider our positions.

What is our Best Position? (BP)

Our dream position, the best we could ever hope to obtain.

What is our Target Position? (TP)

Our realistic position.

What is our Walk Away Position? (WAP)

Where we walk away and look at other options.

Remember to have a soft walk away position just in case you change your mind later. Use language like "That is the best we can do today". A hard walk away position leaves no chance of returning to the table.

What is our Alternative Position? (AP)

Alternative position is the cost or the lost opportunity cost to us if we walk away. What will we do instead, what will it cost us. It is sometimes known as a BATNA, Best Alternative To a Negotiated Agreement.

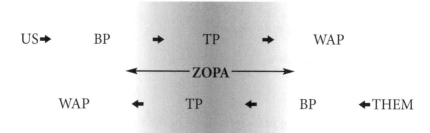

We need to understand these positions, both our position and the position of the other side. Where our positions overlap is the Zone of Potential Agreement (ZOPA). Put yourself in their shoes. Imagine their position. Pretend you are sitting in their office discussing the situation. How do they feel? How important is it to them? Are careers at stake? Are bonuses at stake? Are reputations at stake? What else might be at stake? Where do we think their BP – TP – WAP – AP are?

- What are our variables?

- What are their variables?

- Where are our deal breakers?

- What are their deal breakers?

Get as much information as you can. Information is power. The more information you have, the more options you have.

"Don't wait for the tide to go out before you discover who is swimming naked"

— Harvey Mackay

Agendas

As part of the formal preparation stage for any negotiation, it is a very sensible idea to prepare an agenda. A well prepared agenda is vital to a good negotiation. When preparing your agenda you should consider carefully the following questions:

1. What are you going to discuss and in what order?

2. What are you going to start with?

3. What issues are to be included?

4. What will be omitted?

5. What is the most important issue?

However...

There are other important issues to consider when thinking about agendas.

Everyone's map is different as the psychologists say. Everyone has a different view of the world, the current situation and the situation they personally face.

So consider:

1. What is our agenda?

2. What is the agenda of the other side?

3. Are there any other parties involved like third parties, agents?

4. What hidden agendas, personal agendas are there?

5. What items should we put on or leave off the formal agenda?

6. What items might we brief the "boss" or the experts on, to deal with outside the meeting?

7. Where should we put the controversial items?

8. How much time have we got?

9. How much time have they got?

The difficult items go towards the end.

It is important to get momentum quickly, to avoid getting stuck on specific issues early in the negotiation.

A good opening agenda item might be 'background' as this may encourage the other side to open up with information unknown to you.

Send agendas to the other side early – asking them if they have anything to add. That way you might find out about issues that were unknown to you and give you the chance to do some extra research.

Do your preparation and expect issues of complaint to be raised and be prepared.

Some final thoughts to think about

- Soften up the other side in advance to reduce expectations. Start mentioning issues to reduce their expectations.
- The best negotiators spend at least five times more time planning than average ones.
- Sleep on your plan before putting it into action.
- Ask great questions.
- Listen to the answers.

Plan who you need at the meeting, plan the situation in advance and plan how you will play the agenda.

When IBM had many major computer main frame contracts with the largest of corporations. It used to start its preparation for the next negotiation as it signed off the latest contract. There could have been four years between contracts. They could have had up to 40 people on each client relationship.

We are always negotiating, so we must always be preparing.

Fail to prepare – prepare to fail

Power Tips

- Proper preparation prevents pretty poor performance
- Calculate your positions – BP – TP – WAP - AP
- Consider their positions – BP – TP – WAP – AP
- What are both sides really trying to achieve?

Sometimes you should walk away if the results are not going to be worth the trouble, the hassle or the stress.

"There are three sides to any argument.
Mine, yours and the right one"

— Anon

5. Notes

5. Notes

6

First impressions in negotiating

You don't get a second chance to make a 1st Impression

When I heard the researchers at Harvard saying that the first 10 minutes of any negotiation are crucial to the way it would turn out, I wasn't surprised.

They had worked on resolving crucial issues around the world since the Harvard Negotiating Project was set up in the late 1980's.

Human beings have an innate sense of danger. The part of our brain that defends us is called the reptilian brain, and operates in a nano-second. Are we in danger? Is this person like me, or are they not like me?

Is this team working with us for mutual benefit or have they got their own agenda and will take advantage of us if our guard is down?

We form these impressions and it is hard to change our mind.

Impressions are like quick drying cement, once formed they are very difficult to change.

One to one impressions are often formed in a split second.

I visited a firm of head hunters in London and they told me that they form an impression of a candidate in a split second.

They always meet the candidates at the lift so they are taken by surprise and they typically would look for:

- Eyes – for energy and attitude.
- Smile - for genuineness and positivity.
- Handshake – for touch and feel.
- Shoes - for cleanliness.

Now there is clearly more to this, however dress, grooming and accessories all give us an insight into the other person and the other team, how they may or may not behave.

We all analyse people in a split second, even if we don't realise it. From the way they come across, the way they look, the way they sound - in fact through all our senses.

That is why we often say "Does this make sense?"

Some people say, "It doesn't look right to me", others say, "It doesn't sound right", and some say, "It doesn't feel right."

"Research into criminal trials show that jurors make their mind up about the accused in the first ten minutes and it is very difficult to change their minds."

— The Economist

Let's imagine a negotiation that you are going to be involved in.

What's the 1st impression that you are going to make?

Score yourself on a scale of 0 (Poor) to 10 (Excellent): ......

Think about what you need to do to become a 10.

Now consider:

- What impression does your team make?

- What impression does your company make?

I was working for a company who had negotiation issues, when they had visited South Korea and Japan. They told me that no one had advised them what to do with greetings and with business cards in Japan.

In Japan a business card is an extension of the person. You exchange cards very formally, with two hands on the card and the other person takes it with two hands and admires the card.

In eastern cultures status is very important. You should acknowledge people in order of their status. The management will sit at the meeting in order of seniority.

What my client had done was put their business cards on the table and slid them across the table to the Japanese executives. They had not admired the cards in return. One of the party had made notes on one of the Japanese cards. That should never happen; it is an insult to the other person in Japan and not a good start to a negotiation.

Here are some impression management, preparation questions:

- What is on the agenda?

- Should I send it in advance?

- What do I need to do to be professional?

- Before I leave home, leave the office, do I have everything I need?

- Am I groomed properly?

- Do I have the right accessories, nice pen, notebook, briefcase etc?

- Have I dressed for success?

- How am I going to make sure I am in the right mental state?

- What time should I arrive?

- How should I build rapport at the reception?

- What small talk do I need to build rapport?

- Should I remain standing to be in the right frame of mind?

- What questions do I have? How will I listen?

- How will I follow up?

When I am introduced, when I introduce myself remember to be positive, smiling, pleased to be there.

Make sure my handshake is firm, positive, equal to their power and at a neutral angle?

Seating

Will we sit appropriately for a win, win, win? Sit round the table if possible, be careful about sitting opposite, which has the feel of them and us –Win / Lose.

My friend John makes a judgement about people he meets from their handshakes. A dominant hand on top with a strong grip tells him the person is perhaps highly competitive and wants to win at all costs.

He believes this intuitive judgement gives him an insight into how the person will negotiate and how he should position his first offer. And as you might have guessed he positions the offer high, and he then lets this person negotiate him down;

John gets good deals.

A delegate on a course I ran told me that he was going to a key negotiation in Chicago. His boss told him that he had to shave off his beard before he went as it would give the wrong impression (he had had his beard for 21 years and his wife loved it).

He knew it was the right thing to do and that the beard had held him back in several job negotiations. However here is the funny thing, when he got to Chicago, the representative from the other side had a beard. He couldn't believe what had happened.

(The problem with a beard is the other person cannot see your facial micro gestures very well, and therefore might form the impression that they can't trust you.)

Power Tips

- You never get a second chance to make a first impression.

- Make sure you understand the cultural issues which might cause offence.

- Don't forget to make sure you look, sound and feel good for the circumstances.

6. Notes

6. Notes

7

Asking the right questions

*The quality of the questions you ask determines
the quality of the answers that you get*

Ask ask ask

The ability to ask high quality questions and then accurately listen
to the response is an essential skill.

High quality questions take careful preparation. Under pressure,
without preparation, it is usually difficult to ask the real well
constructed tough questions, in a gentle non offensive way. The
questions that will seek out the answer you need to hear to
determine the truth.

Observing carefully means listening carefully, watching the
accompanying body language for congruence and noticing what is
not said.

The use of high quality questions (HQQ) and active disciplined
listening (ADL) in a negotiation is vital to getting the right
answers to make informed decisions.

Using these two skills together can make all the difference.
Yet many negotiators ask poor questions and therefore get
poor answers.

This chapter will show you how to ask really good questions and to listen to the meaning of the answers you get.

Asking

Some people are afraid to ask, afraid to embarrass the other person, afraid to embarrass themselves or just afraid of the answer they might get.

Always remember:

- If you don't ask you don't get.

- If you don't ask you don't give the other person the opportunity to say yes.

- If you don't ask then the answer will be no.

The real skill is how you ask. Ask nicely, softly and gently assertive.

Don't assume - ASK

In my experience, average negotiators often assume answers to questions, rather than asking the other side. Even if you are pretty sure of the answer it can be beneficial to hear the answer from the other side.

The first three letters of the word assumption are ASS.

Assumptions can make an ASS out of U and ME

If there is any doubt where the other side is coming from, ask, don't assume anything.

When you are asking you are:

Always Seeking Knowledge (ASK)

Types of questions to ask

1. Open questions

Asking quality open questions will seek out long answers, which tend to explain where the other side is coming from.

> *"I keep six honest serving men; they taught me all I knew.*
> *Their names are What and Why and When and How*
> *and Where and Who"*

— Rudyard Kipling

Use Rudyard Kipling's questions as your guide to how to prepare open questions. I prefer to have what and how at the top of my list as these make power questions.

Here are some examples of high quality open questions:

- How much have you got in your budget?

- What is it you need?

- How can we solve this problem?

- How much can you pay?

- How does that work?

- How did it happen like that?

- Who was there?

- Who authorized the schedule?

- Who are the key people?

- Where do you think we are going with this?

- Where were you on that night?

2

Key Secrets

- Where should we start our preparation?

and

- How close can you get to our price?

Here are some more questions that can follow open questions to obtain more information:

- Could you tell me more about..........?

- Can you run that past me again........?

- Please expand on that........

Perhaps just by saying "anything else?" with an enquiring voice tone.

- What do we need to achieve?

- What do you want to achieve here?

- How do you see the outcome?

- What are the issues?

- Why is it an issue?

- Why should we spend any more time on this?

- Why is it that we should do this deal?

- What happened at the meeting?

- What did the client say?

- What is your interpretation of the schedule?

2. Closed questions

Closed questions are those that give you a yes or no answer. Careful use of them should be employed. The danger is that a closed question can allow the other person to avoid the real question.

Remember most quality questions are short, succinct and to the point.

The skill is choosing the question carefully and then keeping quiet. Saying nothing more, until you get an answer.

It is important to remain silent after these questions and wait patiently for the answers.

The longest silences I have heard about are

- Nine hours in a union negotiation.

- Four hours thirty minutes in the Korean War peace negotiations.

Try sitting in silence with someone you don't know very well for 30 seconds and see how awkward that feels.

Ten seconds can seem a long time in some situations; how did these groups manage many hours?

One mistake that is often made is after the quality question is asked; the person does not hold the silence. They go on and ask a supplementary question or make a statement which qualifies the previous question.

This qualification often comes from natural embarrassment for the person who is being questioned. Don't make that mistake. You are now heading toward being a master negotiator.

Good questions coax lengthy and detailed explanations from the other person. If the person cuts the answer short, encourage them, with encouraging nods, ums and supportive questions like, 'anything else?'

If we listen with our two eyes AND our two ears then we get better information to make our judgements.

Often we can keep the conversation going with nods and words such as "yes", "I understand", "keep going", supportive "ums" – which are called "prompters" designed to keep things moving. They should be accompanied with positive and supportive body language.

3. *Why* questions

Why questions have to be more carefully chosen as they can be seen as a personal attack by the receiver. For example:

- Why did you speak to her like that?

- Why did you do that deal?

- Why did you make that decision?

- Why did you forget to call me?"

The person might think, "why are you challenging me?" and we might be in a defensive negative loop if we are not careful.

A friend of mine, Barry, in his training to be a counsellor for the Samaritans was told never to ask "why" to the people who called the helpline. It might be a tipping point for them. For example, to ask, "Why are you feeling so depressed?" might reinforce their negative problem and build it up in their mind.

Why questions can be reframed into more gentle, phrases such as, "tell me about the issues?"

Structure your questions carefully. By structuring your questions you can control the agenda, the meeting and eventually the outcome.

Yes and No tag questions

Yes – tag questions

Yes tag questions are designed to encourage the person to agree with you and build rapport. Sometimes they are used in threes as this can be even more effective. Misused they can be seen to be manipulative.

With *Yes tag* questions even if the person doesn't verbally say yes, they will more often than not think yes in their mind and even nod.

Only ask *Yes tag* questions where you anticipate the majority of people will agree. *Yes* answers tend to create positive momentum.

Examples of Yes Tag questions

- It is a fantastic day, *isn't it?*

- We have made considerable progress, *haven't we?*

- That was a great meal, *wasn't it?*

- We are going to celebrate our success, *aren't we?*

No - Tag questions

No - tag questions can be used to ascertain whether anything else needs to be answered; before moving on to the next stage of a discussion or closing a negotiation. What *No - tag* questions achieve is to get either a 'No' or a 'Yes' answer or alternatively

2

Key Secrets

unsure body language which gives you the opportunity to probe further.

Examples of 'No tag' questions

- Is there anything else you need to know before we go ahead?

- Is there any more research we need to do before we finalise our thoughts?

- Is there further preparation we need to do on the structure of the question before we meet the client tomorrow?

Remember when you get that unsure body language; keep digging with further questions like:

- You don't look too sure....?

- You don't sound like you have cracked it yet?

- Are you really sure?

- It doesn't feel like we have all the answers yet?

- Are you OK with it?

And remember to follow up – to make sure you have the real answers.

A few years ago I was working in risk management for a major international bank. We were concerned about the whereabouts of several million pounds of pension fund assets. One of my colleagues, Peter, was sent to interview a charismatic character who was known for his aggressive financial dealings and his bullying nature.

Peter went to see him face to face and ask him if there were any issues with the company pension fund. He asked him directly whether there was any money missing from the fund. A closed question, requiring only a 'yes' or a 'no' answer.

The charismatic character answered

"That would be illegal Peter, wouldn't it?" in an assertive, dominating and firm tone of voice. My colleague said he was mesmerised with the answer, agreed it would be illegal and failed to follow up. He went away with an uncomfortable "gut feeling" as he had failed to resolve the problem.

He regrets to this day not following up further as it was found out a few days later that millions of pounds were missing from the pension fund.

> *If you ask high quality questions you tend to find the right answers.*

Always remember, average negotiators ASSUME answers that may or may not be right.

Appearing on a radio programme recently I was accused by the presenter of being too nice to be a good negotiator. I explained that the most powerful questions can be asked softly. This was wasted on the interviewer who wanted to make a point that he thought to be a good negotiator you had to sound tough. You don't if you ask high quality questions and probe.

2

Key Secrets

Power Tips

- Prepare and structure your questions in advance.

- Open questions are really powerful and generally start with: *What* or *How*.

- If you don't get a satisfactory answer, re-ask the question in a different way – gently.

7. Notes

7. Notes

8
Listening

Most people need a good listening to
– not a good talking to

Listen is an anagram of SILENT.

To listen accurately you have to remain silent with your outer voice (what you are saying) and your inner voice (what you are thinking).

Silent in your mind means:

- Not thinking about what you are going to say next.

- Not thinking about how you are going to respond.

- Not thinking about distractions. We are of course always surrounded by potential distractions.

Some people think listening skills are easy. This is far from the truth. Active listening needs concentration and total focus. The average person speaks at around 150 to 200 words a minute. However, as some people can think at up to 2000 words a minute this leaves a lot of space for head-chatter in our mind.

'Headchatter' is our inner thoughts, distracting us when we should be listening to someone else.

Lazy Language and Lazy Listening

We often distort what we read, hear and see to make it fit in with our expectations. We delete, distort and generalise information so that it becomes disconnected from its real meaning.

An example of lazy listening might be to ask someone:

"How many animals of each species did Moses take into the Ark?"

More often than not people will answer "two" to this question.

Here is an example of deleting information and assuming that we know the answer as we hear, "How many animals of each species….." and from that moment on, stop listening because we think we know the answer from our previous experiences.

Maybe you are thinking the answer is two, even now.

However you know Moses had nothing to do with the Ark. It was Noah who took two of each species into the Ark! I don't think I needed to tell you that did I? In this example people assume they know what we are going to say and think that listening further is unnecessary.

Listening is one of those skills that we are rarely taught. It is one of those skills that we use all the time but without instruction.

In a recent survey of US sales people, the best ones were not the best speakers, they were the best listeners.

Is there a difference between hearing and listening?

- Hearing is the words.
- Listening is the meaning.

Listen as if your life depends on it. Everybody wants someone else to listen to them.

Before you start listening you should put yourself in a heightened state of awareness. This means that first you have to stop that inner voice talking to you and concentrate 100% on the other person.

A friend of mine says that some people should do some 'ear sharpening' so that they can become a good listener. What he means is they need to sharpen their awareness to listening.

Listening to somebody without passing judgment is a great skill.

Listening is a choice. We generally choose to listen because:

- The message is important.

- We are interested.

- We feel like listening.

- We listened to this type of information in the past.

Three keys to hearing the message:

- Pay attention.

- Select what is important.

- Recognize the emotional messages.

Finally – remember to ask yourself to WAIT

W.A.I.T. stands for, "Why Am I Talking?"

You can't listen and talk – when you find yourself talking – ask yourself

WHY AM I TALKING?

> *"Silence is golden, but my eyes still see"*
>
> — The Tremeloes, 1967 (1m selling single)

Here are just a few reasons why we might be distracted from listening effectively:

- We naturally think we are the most important person in the world. So it is natural to be preoccupied with our own thoughts.

- Often something the other person says can trigger other thoughts in our mind.

- Anchors and triggers are programmed into us by the experiences of life. Something someone says or does can remind us of something that happened to us in the past and start a train of thought in our mind.

- Listening to someone else can be boring, if we decide to think of it that way.

- Listening is an active state not a passive state.

Be careful about saying things for effect. Stay quiet and listen.

Some really good tips for listening

- Set yourself a goal to listen at the start of the meeting.

- Sit with positive, open body language.

- Have a note pad and make short notes.

- Use your eyes and ears. Nod and make positive "umming" noises.

- Ask questions to keep the conversation and discussions on track to where you want them to go. Use the rapid repeat method. Repeat what the other person is saying in your mind.

- Be interested.

- Reduce headchatter. When it comes, be aware of it and ignore it.

- Reduce distractions. Turn off your phone, shut down your computer and any other unnecessary equipment.

- Ensure you have no interruptions.

As I write this many governments are thinking about how they might have to change laws relating to juries. It has been discovered that jurors have lost the ability to listen with all the distractions of the internet, television and all the other 21st century distractions. The Lord Chief Justice in the United Kingdom said "We have a generation now in the jury box, totally unused to sitting and listening. That changes the whole tradition of aurality with which we are familiar". Researchers are suggesting that jurors might be given screens to take away and they might be able to press buttons to obtain information that they wanted clarification on.

The Limited Perception Story.

Listening means interpreting information and asking more questions to check the facts are right. I like the message in this story:

The story is said to be based on an actual radio conversation between a U.S. Navy aircraft carrier (U.S.S. Abraham Lincoln) and the Canadian authorities off the coast of Newfoundland in October, 1995. (The radio conversation was released by the Chief of Naval Operations on 10/10/95 authorized by the Freedom of Information Act, Washington)

It was a foggy evening and shortly after dark, the lookout on the wing of the bridge reported "Light, bearing on the standard bow".

"Is it steady or moving astern" the captain called out.

"Steady captain." Which meant the ship was on a dangerous collision course. At that point a radio message came through from the Canadians.

Canadians: "Please divert your course 15 degrees to the South to avoid a collision."

Americans: "Recommend you divert your course 15 degrees to the North to avoid a collision".

Canadians: "Negative. You will have to divert your course 15 degrees to the South to avoid a collision."

Americans: "This is the Captain of a US Navy ship. I say again, divert YOUR course."

Canadians: "No, I say again, you divert YOUR course."

Americans: "This is the aircraft carrier USS Lincoln, the second largest ship in the United States' Atlantic Fleet. We are accompanied by three destroyers, three cruisers and numerous support vessels.

I demand that you change your course 15 degrees North. I say again, that's one five degrees North or counter measures will be undertaken to ensure the safety of this ship."

The reply came back:

Canadians. "This is a lighthouse – your call"

Asking great questions and listening carefully to the answers will hopefully avoid these types of mistakes

Power Tips

- Listen carefully. You will be surprised what you hear.

- Listen is an anagram of 'silent'. Listen by remaining silent in your head and with your mouth. Take care with your headchatter.

- Make sure you are listening to what the other person is really saying, the real message.

8. Notes

....
....
....
....
....
....
....
....
....
....
....
....
....
....
....
....
....
....
....
....
....

9
Sensory awareness

Does it look right, sound right, feel right, smell right and taste right?

Does it make sense?

High achieving negotiators are able to see, hear, feel and sense what others miss. Higher achievers seem to have cultivated an ability to heighten their sensory acuity or sensory awareness. Some people might call this having high emotional intelligence. This means heightening our awareness, to important things that are going on around us.

Leonardo Da Vinci is popularly quoted as being the first person to have said:

The average person

Looks without seeing

Listens without hearing

Touches without feeling

Smells without awareness

Eats without tasting

You are probably above average as you have invested your time and money in reading this book. However, the more you practice the more you will notice.

Writing things down has the uncanny effect of locking them into your unconscious brain ready for when you need them.

Try this experiment:

Sit in a comfortable chair. Put your right foot out with your foot pointing forward.

Turn your foot in a clockwise direction.

Now put your right hand in the air with your index finger pointing out, and draw the number 6.

Try to keep your foot turning clockwise.

I have tried this exercise on my workshops and seminars for several years. 99% of people find that they cannot keep the foot turning clockwise whilst the finger is turning anti-clockwise making the 6 figure. Why is this?

The hand is connected more closely to the brain than the foot. The foot follows the movement of the hand. Therefore the hand and foot move in unison and the hand wins. What can we learn from this? We need to coordinate our mind and body in the most effective way.

If you are using this book to gather information about negotiating, you might consider making notes to cement the key parts in your unconscious mind, for later. The hand brain connection is strong, stronger than most people imagine. Some employers used to use graphology to help in the selection process for jobs. Graphology is the analysis of handwriting.

Try this experiment:

How many F's can you count in this sentence?

FINISHED FILES ARE THE RESULT OF YEARS

OF SCIENTIFIC STUDY AFTER YEARS OF PRACTICAL APPLICATION

Even though there is no trick here people get different answers. The answer is at the end of this chapter. Some people only see three, four or five F's.

This shows that vital information which is staring us in the face is often missed. In this exercise some people speed read and miss the F's in the 'ofs', others don't pay attention.

The Invisible Gorilla

There is a book written by Dr Richard Wiseman, a UK psychologist, called *Did you spot the Gorilla?*. The title is based on a piece of research conducted at the Harvard Business School by psychologist Dr David Simons.

A video clip is shown to the audience in which two teams of basketball players are passing the basketball to each other.

The audience is asked to count the number of times one of the teams passes the ball. Because they focus on this, the majority of people don't notice a person in a gorilla suit walk across the screen. It's amazing.

Many people have seen the clip as it has been shown on television round the world and played on the internet. Many of the people who have seen it before still fail to see the gorilla.

For a copy go to www.viscog.com

The reason is that they are so busy focusing on something else, counting the passes, that they fail to notice the distraction.

This happens in real life and particularly in negotiations. People get so focused on the deal that they miss all the other information which is available that might make them change their mind, change the price or change the terms and conditions.

Take a little time to raise your awareness to what is going on around you. You will be surprised by the results you will get.

How old is the woman?

Some people see a young woman, some people see the older woman. Perceptions are different. Who did you see?

OPPORTUNITYISNOWHERE

Did you see…?

OPPORTUNITY IS NO WHERE

or did you see…

OPPORTUNITY IS NOW HERE

Answer to the F's in the sentence a couple of pages before. There are seven Fs in the sentence.

Power Tips

- Watch things that are happening around you, it will improve your negotiating.
- Switch your sensory acuity on, "your radar".
- Notice and note things to remember them.

Good negotiators tend to have higher awareness of what is going on around them.

9. Notes

....
....
....
....
....
....
....
....
....
....
....
....
....
....
....
....
....
....
....
....
....
....

10
Reading body language

"It is a staggering five times more difficult to lie with your body language than it is with the words"

— Dr David Lewis, author and psychologist

A man walks into a bar and gets a beer. He looks around and sees four men and a dog playing cards. Astonished, he walks over and watches the game. He then said to one of the players, "That must be the smartest dog in the world, being able to play cards like that." The player looks at the man and says, "Nah, he's not that smart, when he gets a good hand, he wags his tail!"

Do you wag your tail?

You are negotiating with this lady – what does her body language tell you about how you are getting on?

(Answer at end of chapter)

Why is reading body language difficult? It isn't, but people tend to ignore it and rely on what is said.

Body language helps us to understand what people are thinking and really mean by reading their gestures.

It is vital that we observe, interpret and check the non-verbal signals we are receiving to ensure they match the verbal evidence. The body and the mind are inseparable; how we think shows somewhere in our physical micro-expressions (small usually facial expressions that we would not consciously see). By raising our awareness we stand a much higher chance of not being misled.

It is said that only one person in a hundred is proficient at reading and interpreting body language. Yet 93% of the information we receive comes from sources other than the actual words. You need to know how your body language comes across to others in important circumstances. You could be giving away vital information.

Body language skills relate directly to the sub-conscious workings of the brain. Therefore, we may not consciously notice the signals we are receiving. If you raise your conscious awareness and look for tell tale signals, you will become a much better negotiator.

Research into the impact of communication skills shows the following breakdown of how we receive or interpret the information:

Only **7%** comes from **the words**: what is actually said

With **38%** from the **tone of voice** the way it is said

And **55%** from the silent speech signals: **the Body Language**

This means that during a typical exchange; whether it is a casual conversation, an intimate encounter, a vital job interview, or a delicate and crucial negotiation, more than half the information available will be visual rather than verbal.

Take care - when you are negotiating on the phone you need to concentrate 100% to hear the real meaning of what the other person is saying, as there is no available body language to see.

There are many reasons why body language signals are ignored and some of these are:

- There is so much information we filter the visuals.

- We find it easier to concentrate on the left brain logical skills of the words.

- We get anxious / stressed during the discussions, which makes us tense and we don't use our right brain observation skills, which interpret visual information.

- We are lazy.

Researchers have found it is five times more difficult to disguise what you mean or what you really believe with your body language than it is with your words. This is why professional 'liars' such as politicians and lawyers have considerable training in concealing their visual gestures.

Body language is a mixture of 'clusters' that should be looked at in the circumstances which prevail at the time. One signal on its own can be very misleading; it is the clusters that must be interpreted.

For example, folded arms can indicate someone is feeling cold. Alternatively if someone folds his or her arms in response to something you have just said you can interpret that as a negative response to your suggestion.

Wise negotiators would pick this up immediately and either change tack or challenge the response, depending on the circumstances.

Body language needs to be interpreted in clusters, based on combinations of the following:

- Personal appearance

- Eye contact and movement

- Facial expressions

- Hands, arms, legs and other body gestures

- Bodily posture

- Spatial awareness

Reading body language is intuitive and common sense.

The problem with common sense is that it is not as common as it used to be!

I recommend taking an observer to an important negotiation with the sole job of watching the body language and getting a gut/intuitive feel of the meeting. At the break or adjournment, seek the views of the observer before proceeding. You might be amazed at what they have seen.

Improve your own skill by watching people in a coffee shop, a bar or an airport, and see what you intuitively pick up about their conversations. Alternatively, turn the sound down on a television programme and watch for 15 minutes in silence. You will be surprised at your level of understanding. Watch politicians with the sound turned down and you will be surprised at what you see.

Can you tell who this man is speaking to in each telephone box?

It has been suggested; one is his wife, one is his lover and one is his boss. From the body language can you tell? Answer at the end of the chapter.

"Every time he told a lie, Pinocchio rubbed his nose"

— Walt Disney

At a re-financing of a loan deal, the Treasurer of a multi-national television company was asked to confirm that the company could repay the loan at expiry. As he said it was possible, he rubbed his nose several times.

When people say things that they don't believe are necessarily true they often get a tingling feeling around the sensitive part of the nose, which they unconsciously rub.

Watch out for nose rubbing. When you see it re-ask the question in a different way; watch and listen to the answer, before you make your judgement.

Power Tips

- Focus on the importance of reading and interpreting the body language.

- The truth is often disguised in the non-verbal signals.

- It is the combination of what is said and the body language clusters that need to be interpreted.

Answers to puzzles:

Lady with arms folded: How are you getting on? Not very well. She is frowning, narrowing her eyes, pouting her lips and folding her arms. None of which are good body language signs for a deal.

Telephone box: 1 - Office, 2 - Wife, 3 - Lover.

10. Notes

10. Notes

....

....

....

....

....

....

....

....

....

....

....

....

....

....

....

....

....

....

....

....

....

....

11
The truth about lying

The more information you have to interpret the facts, the better decisions and judgements you can make

Deception

> *"You can't hide your lying eyes.*
> *And your smile is a thin disguise, thought by now you'd realise,*
> *there ain't no way to hide your lying eyes"*
>
> — Lying eyes, The Eagles, 1975

Deceivers and liars give themselves away in many subtle ways – trust your intuition. If it seems too good to be true, it probably is…

Deception comes in many forms. Recognising the basic signs can be very helpful to your decision-making, your time management and your business focus. When people are lying, uncomfortable or nervous the stress manifests itself somewhere in their non-verbal signals.

Stress does not mean someone is lying. However, we need to recognise that it might, and make our judgements accordingly.

Stress can be seen at the extremities; our hands and our feet. Feet bobbing, hand movements, fidgeting gestures and dilated pupils might all suggest a degree of discomfort including lying.

Body language deception gestures can be a combination of things. Look for an increase in hand to face gestures. In research undertaken in California, nurses who were told to give patients positive news that was untrue; had ten times more hand to face gestures than when they knew they were telling the truth.

If you notice more hand to face gestures than normal - be on your guard

Professional liars will have learnt how to handle situations where they choose not to tell the truth. There tend to be fewer gestures, fewer body movements and sometimes more eye contact than you would expect.

I worked with Dr Wiseman at the University of Hertford and we also spoke at several conferences together. His research into lying shows, like many similar studies, that good liars can often fool people with their body language. Whereas when you cannot see them (you are listening to a recording in sound only) the truth is often easier to detect.

Some years ago Dr Wiseman won a competition to try an experiment on Tomorrows World television programme. He recorded two interviews which were shown to a TV audience, played on the radio and the transcript was written in the newspapers. In the interviews a journalist, Sir Robin Day was asked to lie in one clip and tell the truth in another. The subject was his favourite film. He was also asked to conceal what was in fact his favourite film. 72% of the radio audience got the correct film whereas only 52% of the TV viewers were correct. The TV viewers were fooled by the deception in the body language. 64% of the newspapers readers were correct.

Police forces often listen just to audio recordings of the interviews as without the visual distractions they can form a more accurate picture of what really happened.

Linguistic deception

According to Dr Wiseman linguistic deception comes in the form of a slowing down of the speech rate. An increase in the voice pitch together with an increase in *ahs, ums* etc. more slips and mistakes and delays in responses.

We all intuitively know that liars avoid eye contact so be careful when people over compensate to show they are telling the truth by holding extra eye contact.

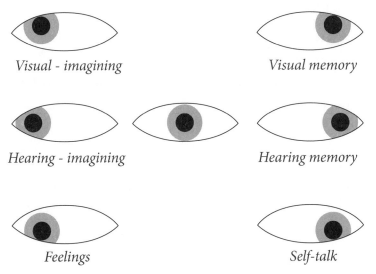

Visual - imagining   Visual memory

Hearing - imagining   Hearing memory

Feelings   Self-talk

Eye Accessing Cues

Eye accessing cues can also be very helpful when assessing

2
Key Secrets

whether people are telling the truth or not. 80% of people look up and to the left, when they are accessing something that actually happened in the past. They look up and to the right, when they are imagining an event that might happen in the future or inventing something that didn't happen in the past. The other 20% of people look in the other direction, which is why it is important to establish a person's preference at the beginning.

In the movie 'The Negotiator' there is a scene where Kevin Spacey screams "I know you are lying because your eyes moved to the right"

When I am interviewing someone for a client and trying to find out whether they are telling the truth, I will ask a control question first such as "What is your Mother's maiden name?", and see which way the eyes move, to know which way they move when they are telling the truth. Then ask the question I really want answered and watch the reaction of the eyes.

Many police forces use this as part of their interviewing procedures. However, there is no country at present where this has been introduced as acceptable evidence in a court of law. These eye movements need to be combined with the verbal information to give us a good insight to where the truth lies.

Words

Check that the words someone uses today match what you have been told before. Intuitively we know when someone is not being entirely honest. People have a habit of being incongruent in some way which is not picked up consciously.

They leak dishonesty somewhere and our unconscious mind is like a magnet that picks up the information.

"He's a blinking liar"

People who are uncomfortable with what they are saying can increase their blink rate by up to four times.

Here is an exercise you might like to do with a colleague or a friend. It is very good for raising your sensory acuity to deception.

Sit down with the other person opposite you. Tell them that you are going to think about someone you like and try to disguise your body language. Then you are going to think about someone you don't like and try to disguise your body language. See if they can notice the difference. Usually there will be small micro gestures around the face and eyes which will be different.

Now think of these two people several times in different orders and challenge your friend to tell you which one is which, by watching your body language. Then reverse it and let them practice on you.

2

Key Secrets

Power Tips

- Your gut feeling can be a very good guide.

- If you think someone has told you a lie, ask them a similar question a couple of minutes later.

- Always keep alert to being deceived.

11. Notes

Section 3:

Tactics and Strategies
for Power Negotiating

- **Tactics, manoeuvres and ploys**

- **The power of influencing**

- **The psychology of bargaining**

- **How to haggle**

- **How to handle conflict**

- **The benefits of team negotiations**

3
Tactics and Strategies

12

Tactics, manoeuvres and ploys

What is the purpose of a negotiation tactic?

A negotiation tactic is used to change the perception of power, in the minds of the other side. In simple terms, it is played to get you down to your walk away position as quickly as possible.

Recognising a tactic for what it is, neutralising it and continuing towards your goal is paramount.

People like to play games. Sometimes games are fun sometimes games are dangerous and sometimes people get hurt. Tactics can be similar. Properly used tactics can help to ensure that people make up their minds to take action. Badly used they can trick people into doing things that they should never do.

As a master negotiator you need to understand tactics, how they can be used for everyone's advantage, how you can spot them and how to flush them out.

Tactics are used to change the other person's perception of where the power lies and unless you are aware it is a ploy, it may work.

3

Tactics and Strategies

Tactics or ploys or gambits, as they are called in different parts of the world, come in three distinct categories:

1. Ethical tactics

2. Marginal tactics

3. Unethical or dirty tactics

Whilst it is difficult to categorise anything without making generalisations, I have tried to make distinctions.

Ethical tactics, some of which are mentioned in the next chapter on influencing skills, are psychological manoeuvres to help people make up their minds. Many people need help making their minds up on occasions which is fine as long as it is a good decision and it makes sense.

On the other hand dirty tactics will only have one outcome, "win / lose", and "win / lose" has it's own consequences.

Perceptions

The success of a negotiation depends very much on the power of the respective parties. It is the perception of where the power lies that is important. Skilled negotiators can change the perception of the power by the expert use of tactics.

We have to accept and deal with tactics being used on us. At the same time, when necessary, we may employ ethical tactics ourselves to gain competitive advantage. For example the use of a time deadline can help people make up their minds instead of procrastinating.

Train yourself to spot a tactic for what it is, tag it and isolate it. This will dramatically help your success in negotiating.

Top tactics you must be aware of

Good guy - Bad guy (good cop / bad cop)

With two people in a meeting, one person is nice, the other person is aggressive. After a while the aggressive person leaves temporarily and the nice person says "If you can agree to this, this and this then I may be able to get the other person to agree".

The police use this as good cop / bad cop. "If you give me the information I will make sure my colleague backs off with charging you with the other offences that he wants to go for".

In a small business it might be as simple as one partner saying their other partner would never agree, and then asking what else can be given to get agreement.

In a relationship partnership it can be used by saying "My wife / my partner will go crazy if I pay that much, is there something you can do to help me?"

In a large business this might be the relationship / account manager saying to the other side, "I would really like to do this for you. How can you help me get it through the committee / or the board? What else can you give me to sweeten the deal?"

Often people say to me, isn't this a bit manipulative? They forget that usually they are already not making sufficient profit for their efforts and should try to earn more. This is a good tactic to flush out what the other side might be able to pay, and learn the truth.

3

Tactics and Strategies

Higher authority – (I need to talk to my people)

Many people think it shows weakness to say they cannot make the decision on the spot and sometimes agree to deals they later regret.

Master negotiators know that they must always have 'higher authority' in their armoury.

It is powerful to place the blame on someone else for not being able to agree to a request, because it means you can stay in rapport with the other side.
It means that they may alert you to other issues that you have not been aware of.

You can use phrases like, "I would love to say yes, but the committee won't sign it off unless you give me something else."

Try combining good guy / bad guy and higher authority to get better deals

Time

People, who are short of time, tend to make more concessions. 80% of the concessions tend to come in the last 20% of the available negotiating time.

Make sure you are in control of the time, so you do not get pressured to concede on a false time deadline.

Time outs and breaks

When you want to consider an offer from the other side or things seem to have stalled, don't be afraid to ask for a break. This break is often called a time out, an adjournment or going to the balcony.

(going to the balcony is an expression that comes out of the Harvard Research project, when they realised that most negotiators were not stopping to review the situation often enough).

The benefits of taking a time out are threefold:

1. It gives you thinking time. When we are under pressure, often we cannot think rationally and creatively.

2. It tends to take the emotions out of the situation. Gives a chance for either side to calm down and think back to the goal. Separate the people, from the problem.

3. It gives you a chance to talk to your colleagues, who will usually have a different take on the situation. The more minds you have working on the situation, generally the better ideas you will get.

Even if you are on your own, take a few minutes to consider the situation. Write it down on a piece of paper, go through your notes or phone a colleague and talk it through with them. If necessary adjourn for 24 hours, so that you can sleep on it.

Flinching on the price

Flinching is jargon in negotiating, for acting surprised when the other side makes an offer. It comes in all formats. From gentle "your joking" to the more aggressive outrage that some people seem to enjoy.

When someone says, "it costs X", you might simply squint and draw breath before asking, "How much?" in an enquiring, surprised tone of voice.

At the United Nations, during the Cuban missile crisis, President Kruschev of the Soviet Union deliberately banged his shoe on the table to show his surprise and anger to the United States and the other member nations. When they reviewed the recordings of this incident, they noticed that he hadn't taken his shoe off. One of his

3

Tactics and Strategies

aides had passed a spare shoe to him, just at the point before he expressed his anger. It had been pre planned. Act in anger, don't react in anger.

In the early days of my negotiating career I was in Liverpool negotiating with a retailer. They had an assistant treasurer who was known for flinching in an outrageous way whenever price was mentioned. We were ready for his flinch when we named our price. This time he went into his usual rant, threw his chair back and smashed his head into the wall. We were pretty sure he didn't mean to do this and hurt his head. It was really difficult not to smile as we had been expecting this ploy. We didn't concede. We stuck to our plan and got a good deal.

Have an observer to read the body language, the situation and the big picture.

Have someone watch the body language and tell you how they think the other side are going to react when you call a time out. It is very difficult to discuss, trade or argue and watch the body language at the same time. Make sure you take someone with you. When you are under stress or thinking on your feet the left hemisphere of the brain tends to take over. This is the part of the brain that is focused on logic, numbers and detail.

The right side of the brain which sees the body language, the nuances and the big picture does not function so well when you are under pressure. So your observer who is watching and listening can pick up key clues by being in a calm alert state.

Nibbling

Just when you think you have got agreement, the other side comes back and asks for another concession. You may have agreed the price and they then ask for another discount. You may have agreed the delivery date and then they ask for it earlier. You may have agreed the payment terms and then they ask for the money earlier.

Children are fantastic at using this tactic, asking for one thing and when it is agreed, asking for something else. Make sure you have everything on the table and you are clear on what has been agreed. If time is short, write the details on a piece of paper, photocopy the paper and ensure both sides sign it. If they still want something else, ask for something back in return. For example "If we give you this....we need that from you?"

Low balling

Low balling is where an outrageously low offer is made, to lower the other side's expectations and perhaps also to flush out the other side's walk away position (WAP).

Recognise the tactic and show your surprise that clearly they are not serious.

If they put a low price on the table to you. Be careful as they may have to re-negotiate the price higher at a later date. This is often done on building contracts or other highly competitive contracts where the other side assume they are going to upsell you more profitable products once they have the contract and the work has started.

3

Tactics and Strategies

Funny Money

Funny money is where something is priced or a price is reduced to a number which looks like it has been carefully calculated. For example "we can produce this for £9643.00." It may have been carefully calculated or it may have been a judgement. However it may look more realistic than £9500.00 to the other side.

When figures are precise they have verisimilitude (the appearance of truth) and psychologically are regarded as more considered and more calculated. This is often not the case.

Dumb is smart – The Colombo tactic

You pretend you don't understand to make the other side explain what they are asking again. This can be used when you think the other side is not telling you all the truth and you want to get to the bottom of all the facts.

Colombo was the 1970s detective on Television who played the "dumb is smart" role. He never seemed to quite understand what the other side was saying and kept asking questions, that implied he hadn't been listening or he had been distracted. This meant the other person had to explain themselves again, and by doing this often gave extra information away, either in what they said or with their body language.

Car dealers often use what they refer to as the 'Colombo close' if a customer is walking out of the showroom having decided not to buy after a haggle. They might say "I don't know what came over me; I had forgotten but we had an instruction from Head Office this morning that we can discount this car further. I am so stupid I totally forgot about it" or something similar. "Come back, sit down and I will see what else I can do for you"

10   **The Evening Bulletin**

PHILADELPHIA, Friday, April 11, 1969

2 Sides Sit Silently 4½ Hours At Korean Truce Meeting

Panmunjom, Korea – (UPI) – The American general and the North Korean general glared at each other across the table and the only sound was the wind howling across the barren hills outside their hut.

Maj. Gen. James B. Knapp, negotiator for the United Nations Command (UNC), was waiting for Maj. Gen. Ri Choon-sun of the Democratic People's Republic of North Korea to propose a recess.

They sat there, arms folded, for 4½ hours. Not a word. Finally, Gen. Ri got up, walked out and drove away.

It was the 289th meeting of the Korean Military Armistice Commission at the truce village of Panmunjom and set a record as the longest such meeting since the Korean War ended July 27, 1953.

The generals had been there 11 hours and 35 minutes. Neither ate or went to the toilet in all that time. Delegates to such meetings may leave the room only with a formal adjournment proposal.

Whichever side proposes a meeting usually proposes a recess. North Korea called yesterday's session. Ri never did propose a recess.

"In view of North Korea's rude and unwarranted conduct," Knapp said, "I consider this meeting to be terminated."

Before the 4½ hours of silence, Knapp called on North Korea to start a four-step de-escalation to ease tension along the Korean border. He promised reciprocation with a similar UNC program.

Knapp asked that North Korea:

–Remove from the North Korean part of the Demilitarized Zone all illegal weapons and unauthorized personnel.

–Immediately quit all attacks against South Korean and UNC forces.

–Reduce what Knapp said was the excessive size of North Korea's armed forces.

–Discontinue "polemic, bellicose, war-mongering public statements."

3

Tactics and Strategies

Silence

The use of silence after asking a good question is very powerful.

Ask a great question and wait for a response. If you need to help the other side, then do but leave the silence. However never forget your goal is to learn where they are really coming from. So don't let them off the hook, keep probing and remain silent for their response.

Parking issues

Momentum gets things done. Getting stuck on an issue can stall a negotiation. It is much better to get the things we agree on out of the way. Park issues to one side where you have disagreement, and come back to them later. It can be very effective to have agreed eight points and only have two things that we disagree on. "If we can sort one, can you sort the other?"

Softening up

If there is bad news to come out, such as a price rise or a tax rise, it is a very effective tactic to soften the other side up to the bad news early. Governments often do this by leaking information to see the reaction they get from the public and the best way to play it going forward.

Leaking issues

Leaking is used in a similar way to softening up, however it is much less subtle. In the case of political negotiations the information might be leaked to the press. The same can happen with business negotiations. With smaller style negotiations information might be told to someone in confidence who is known for not keeping secrets on the basis they will tell others.

Dirty tactics
– How to swim with the sharks without getting eaten

Harvey Mackay has sold more than 40 million books. His very bestselling book is called 'Swim with the sharks without getting eaten'. This makes a great title for this sub section.

Make sure you are thoroughly prepared, know your objectives, and understand the elements of your proposal / terms.

Don't be naive - some adversarial type negotiators will resort to using dirty tactics all the time. They won't even see them as unethical; they will just see them as part of the game.

Be alert for dirty tactic signals such as extreme demands, no authority, no concessions and threats.

Learn to spot particular ploys that indicate deception, those designed to make you feel uncomfortable and those that lock the other side into their position.

Respond only when you are prepared. If necessary call a "time out". Often just recognising a "dirty tactic" will neutralise it or simply asking a question about a tactic may be enough to get the other party to stop using it.

Stay calm. Avoid taking things personally. Do not get defensive.

Show confidence - do not be intimidated, and be firm.

Test the other party's resolve by asking questions or remaining silent. Do not give any important information away.

3
Tactics and Strategies

Be persistent and maintain the inner desire to achieve your objectives. You may have to work harder and longer at it!

Don't attack the other negotiators personally for using a tactic you consider to be dirty. If they get defensive it may be more difficult for them to give up the tactic, and they may be left with a residue of anger that will fester and interfere with other issues.

Question the tactic, not their personal integrity. Rather than saying, "You deliberately put me here facing the sun," attack the problem: "I am finding the sun in my eyes quite distracting".

If all else fails, be prepared to walk away from the negotiation if it is a 'win / lose' with you on the 'lose' side. You might consider saying, "It's my impression that you may not be interested in negotiating in a manner that we both think will produce results. You have my telephone number call me if you change your mind, but I do have alternative options."

An intimidating scene – using tactics, ploys and gambits

Several years ago I asked two actors to make a short DVD clip. In the clip I got the actors to demonstrate a number of dirty negotiation tactics in a short period of time. The scenario was a supplier coming in to see a major buyer, in the buyer's office.

Here are some of the ploys that were played to intimidate the supplier:

- There was no welcome, no handshake and no greeting.

- The supplier was given a lower chair to sit in.

- The buyer carried on with a phone call and didn't acknowledge the supplier.

- When the call was finished the buyer ignored the supplier and wrote his notes up.

- No drink was offered; the buyer already had one which he drunk in front of the supplier.

- There was no apology for the wait and the buyer got the supplier's name wrong.

- The buyer then explained he had so many companies trying to sell products to him, he couldn't remember everybody's name.

- He then asked if the supplier had the authority to make decisions, without referring back to his boss.

- If the supplier didn't have the authority, he said he wanted to deal with someone who did.

- The buyer then said that on the bid that had been submitted, the company had been:

  - Late with the bid.

  - Hadn't covered all the issues.

  - And the pricing wasn't sharp enough.

    (here he was utilising the power of three)

- Then the buyer got up and came round to the supplier's side of the desk invading his space.

- Sat on the desk looking down.

- Tapped the supplier on the shoulder.

- Said there was no way he could show the bid to his people.

3

Tactics and Strategies

- He then said he had drawn up another contract with his terms and conditions, which he said was approved by his directors.

- So if the supplier would sign it – they could get on with the rest of the business. Implying there was more business to come.

This cameo can be split into a number of sections and whilst it is deliberately humorous and fun, there is a very serious side to it. As a negotiator I have had all the ploys played on me. Luckily not all at the same time!

Breaking the cameo down into sections, we have:

Section 1 – First impression, set up

Greeting and set up were non-existent, buyer was rude.

Extended no courtesies.

Got name wrong.

Put supplier in a low chair.

Offered no refreshments.

Section 2 – The bid

Authority to make decisions was questioned.

Stated bid didn't cover all the issues.

Emphasised it was too expensive, not detailed enough and late.

Section 3 – Personal intimidation

Pen pointing, standing up, invading space.

Re-drawn contract, handing pen to sign.

An indication that they couldn't move on until document signed.

A couple of important points

1. Authority - He asked if the supplier had the authority to make decisions, yet when it came to his authority, he had to get the approval of his directors.

An interesting ploy that some people might use and you must be on your guard against, is to get the other side to admit they have authority and then have to refer to higher authority themselves. This gives the ability to change your offer later but lock the other side in.

2. Power of three – Making points in threes is very powerful. Three has a rhythm and many people have what is known in psychological terms as a three times convincer. If they hear, see or do something three times they are more likely to be persuaded or influenced.

The question is would you really want to do business with someone who behaves like this. If they behave like this normally, what will happen when a problem arises as they invariably do with a product, a delivery issue or payment?

> *"Don't wrestle with a pig"*
>
> — Mark McCormack

Be careful who you deal with, leopards don't change their spots. People tend to negotiate the same way each time.

3 Tactics and Strategies

Power Tips

- Tactics are games people play to reduce your expectations and reduce you to your walk away position quickly.

- Take a time out to think through your options and positions. This is particularly important where you are being pushed into making a decision or when time is short.

- Avoid reacting to the tactic wherever possible.

12. Notes

3 Tactics and Strategies

12. Notes

....
....
....
....
....
....
....
....
....
....
....
....
....
....
....
....
....
....
....

13
The power of influencing

"Today it is not enough to have a good case; it's the good presentation of that case which will get the buy in."

— Dr Robert Cialdini, Regents' Professor Emeritus of Psychology and Marketing, Arizona State University, Phoenix USA

You can link the subtle nuances of influencing that Dr Robert Cialdini has researched and compacted into six strategies, to negotiating tactics. Dr Cialdini's book, *Influence Science and Practice*, has sold 300,000 copies worldwide and was several years ago the bestselling business book in China. His work has been used by people and companies all over the world. He is considered to be the number one authority on how we are psychologically influenced. There are thousands of tactics yet Cialdini has distilled the key sub-conscious influencing skills into just six key strategies.

These strategies work best when you use them to get the CLIMATE (or atmosphere) right before you start to make your case. They are almost as important as the case you make.

3
Tactics and Strategies

The six strategies are:

Liking: Make sure the person likes you. People buy from or are influenced by people they like.

Reciprocation: Giving something unconditionally for nothing.

Scarcity: People want things that are in short supply or they think they might miss out.

Social proof: People want things that other people have, even if there is no logical reason to have it.

Authority: People are more persuaded by trappings, such as dress, certificates, qualifications, accessories etc.

Commitment and consistency: If someone agrees to something, it is very hard to go back on it later.

Strategy 1: Liking

People like people who are like themselves

Build rapport.

Make a conscious decision to do things that result in the other person liking you. Gently match and mirror the language, voice tonality and body language of the people you want to influence. So don't shout at a quiet person and don't be timid with a thick-skinned person.

When you feel you are getting on with someone you can then start to 'lead' by subtly changing these behaviours. This is called pacing and leading.

Flattery works

Be subtle, sensible and genuine in your use of praise and people will like you for your positive observations.

We tend to like people who like us and do the same types of things as us.

> *"The deepest principle in human nature is*
> *the craving to be appreciated"*
>
> — William James 19th century philosopher

Physical attraction

When people are physically attractive, juries tend to be twice as lenient. As 90% of our attractiveness is how we dress, no matter how you feel about your physical shape, if you dress well, groom your hair and look smart, people will be more generous to you.

Be positive

There is a natural tendency to like people who bring us positive news. Positive people bring positive energy and optimism. Conversely there is a tendency to dislike people who bring us bad news.

> *"Don't shoot the messenger"*

The saying don't shoot the messenger, is an interesting phrase. The messenger being the bringer of bad news, usually gets tarnished with the bad news even though it is not their fault.

3 Tactics and Strategies

Strategy 2: Reciprocation

If you give things to other people unconditionally, then they will feel they owe you something in return. The strange thing is that the value of what you give to them bears no resemblance to what they might feel they need to give you in return. Gifts of friendship, kindness, small entertainment, listening when they have issues, all count.

People repay in kind.

In your personal interactions with people, the old phrase, "give and you will receive" really works. Doing things for people that help them, without asking for or expecting a favour returned, makes people feel they owe you a favour back. It is no different in business and is why companies give out free samples.

Another example is when restaurant waiters give customers sweets or mints with their bill, they tend to get bigger tips.

Give without remembering – receive without forgetting

Strategy 3: Scarcity

People want more of things in limited supply. Always highlight your unique benefits and exclusive information.

Here are some examples of scarcity being used in business:

- Offer only available until Saturday.

- Limited edition.

- Only a few dates left in my diary.

- Classic Disney films are to be released again for 3 weeks only.

- My diary is booked up for the next 3 months.

- Sale ends at 5.00pm.

- The meeting must finish by 9.00pm.

Strategy 4: Social Proof

Others have bought it, others have it and others have given to this charity. People follow the lead of people who are like them.

Use peer power whenever it's available.

Beggars get more donations when they have some money (but not too much) already in their begging bowl. In Starbucks the tips box is usually pretty full with small coins and people feel they should give their coins because others have.

TV producers put canned laughter on their shows because it is proven to encourage more people to laugh.

Testimonials from customers in sales letters have been proven to increase response rates, especially when the testimonial includes a photograph of the person, as it is more believable.

Strategy 5: Authority

People defer to experts. Expose your expertise

The main elements are titles, trappings and clothes. Here are examples, scientifically tested, that show how 'trappings' make a difference:

Doctors' advice was more highly thought of when their certificates of qualifications were showing in their practice rooms.

When a luxury car rather than an old car sits at a green traffic light, it takes longer for people behind to honk their horns.

3 Tactics and Strategies

40% of placebos (fake medicine) work if a Doctor administers them with total confidence. This is an amazing statistic and there is a lot of self interest from drug companies and traditional medical people trying to stop research into placebos.

When a respected captain of an aeroplane with engine problems switched off the wrong engine, a co-pilot noticed the error but didn't stand up to the captain. Aviation authorities now give assertiveness training to co-pilots.

Strategy 6 Commitment and Consistency

People align with their clear commitment

When people make their commitments active, public and voluntary, they tend to stick to them because they want to appear consistent.

Get a public commitment from others you are working with using phrases like, "If I do this, will you buy?"

One of the key drivers behind the success of "Weight Watchers" and similar groups is that the members give a public commitment to each other. This makes the commitment very difficult to go back on without losing face.

When a client fills in their own order form they are less likely to change their mind and cancel the order.

Cultural Issues

These power-influencing strategies work worldwide but have different emphasis in different countries.

Stanford University researched, with Citigroup worldwide, this question:-

"If one of your colleagues asked you to work on a big project in what circumstances would you feel the most obligated to help?"

- In Spain - if they knew my family or friends - (liking / trust)
- In the Far East - Hong Kong - if they knew my boss (authority)
- In UK, US and Canada - if they had done something for me before (reciprocity)
- In Germany - If the rules of the company said I should (authority)

Four quotes from Dr Robert Cialdini:

"...opportunities seem more valuable when they are less available..."

*"...if you perceive it to be difficult to get,
you become more motivated to get it!"*

"Arrange the climate in which they prefer to say yes"

"You must be congruent before the client will trust you"

I like meeting people for refreshments in a nice coffee store to discuss deals. It meets a number of Dr Cialdini's principles.

3

Tactics and Strategies

1. You are on neutral ground.

2. The tables are round.

3. I insist on buying the coffee.

4. It doesn't take up much time. It is informal.

5. People generally feel comfortable.

Important note on influencing and bargaining

At this point I want to make a comment about the difference between influencing and bargaining (covered in the next chapter). Here in the influencing chapter we talk about the power of giving something for nothing (reciprocity). Giving unconditionally to build rapport and psychologically to sow the seed that the other person owes you something in return.

In the bargaining chapter, we talk about never giving things for nothing, trading everything. Bargaining is normally where we are actually closing the negotiation, coming to a conclusion, as opposed to influencing the other person. The key words in bargaining are "if you do this for us then we will do that for you". Making the concession conditional.

Power Tips

- Give small things to the other side unconditionally.

- Do everything you can to be liked and look the part.

- Get their commitment to go ahead, if you make a concession.

13. Notes

....

....

....

....

....

....

....

....

....

....

....

....

....

....

....

....

....

....

....

....

3 Tactics and Strategies

13. Notes

....
....
....
....
....
....
....
....
....
....
....
....
....
....
....
....
....
....
....
....

14

The psychology of bargaining

Always trade concessions

If you will do that for us - then we will do this for you

Bargaining

Bargaining tends to be for longer term relationships. If you are involved in a dispute in your private life, or you are buying or selling from friends, relations or a long term supplier, then you are more likely to be bargaining rather than haggling

Bargaining is usually the preserve of long term relationships.

Haggling generally has no ongoing relationship BUT be careful, as people should always be treated with respect. You never know where you might meet that person again.

3 Tactics and Strategies

145

The 10 vital do's and don'ts of Bargaining:

DO:

- **Spend considerable time preparing for the negotiation.**

  Gather information, information is power. Work out your *Best Position*, *Target Position* and *Walk Away Position* before the meeting. Also think carefully about your Alternative Position (what you will do with your resources if you walk away). Establish your objectives and be sure that everyone in your team clearly understands them. Try not to negotiate on the telephone unless you are well prepared.

- **Separate the people from the problem**

  Try to establish the key issues of importance / goals for the other side and concentrate on trading away inexpensive variables which are valuable concessions to the other side.

- **Use silence to good effect. Listen more than talk.**

  Control your emotions. If someone has made an unreasonable demand do not 'rise to the bait' but remain silent for a few seconds. This should cause the other party to reconsider or justify the demand. Make notes if necessary.

- **Make sure that both parties understand what has been agreed.**

  Make notes of concessions gained and granted as you go along. Stop for periodic summaries of the position.

- **Go for a "Win / Win" scenario.**

  Try to reach an amicable, wise and equitable conclusion so that both sides come away with the feeling that they got a good deal.

Seek to strengthen long-term relationships through the negotiation process.

DON'T:

- **Give something for nothing.**

  Trade everything. Make all concessions you give conditional on getting something in return, preferably of a higher value. Use conditional language such as "If you can do X for us then we would be able to do Y for you."

- **Be afraid to ask.**

  If you don't ask you don't get, give yourself room to manoeuvre. Have confidence in the quality of services that you provide and show this confidence to the customer.

- **Be the first to make a major concession.**

  This makes you appear too eager and weakens your position. Minor concessions 'to get the ball rolling' are quite in order. Never accept the first offer.

- **Say "No problem" when giving a concession.**

  Make the other side feel that they have won something of great value whenever you give a concession.

- **"Split the difference"**

  This suggestion often leads to an inequitable result, especially where it is made when the time for negotiation is running out. Take the suggestion as a 50 % concession and negotiate on the other 50 %.

3
Tactics and Strategies

Remember...

HOW you concede is more important than WHAT you concede for preserving long term relationships

"Don't accept the first offer" – *A client of mine bought a property in Sandbanks, Dorset. She made an offer £10,000 under the asking price and the offer was immediately accepted. She spent the next two months worrying that there was something wrong with the property. If the seller had haggled she would not have worried so much!*

Negotiable Variables

Definition - Small inexpensive items that cost one side very little but are more valuable to the other side. Negotiable variables are sometimes called:

- Inexpensive valuable concessions
- BOTTS – bargaining opportunities that are tradeable

or simply...

- Negotiables

In our negotiations and in our businesses we all have variables. Both sides can often think that their variables are not valuable and can often think that the other side's variables are valuable.

When you are bargaining you need to know all your variables.

Having your negotiable variables in mind when you negotiate any situation is a prerequisite of your preparation.

Here are some examples of variables

1. Different types of pricing

Payment terms – 30 days, 60 days, 90 days

Payment date of invoices

Delaying / deferring / bringing forward / part payments

Length of contract

2. Advice

Management time

Site visits

Advice on purchasing, staff issues etc

3. Service

Extras as part of the service

Access outside usual hours - Personal mobile phone numbers (rather than business mobiles) for emergencies or big opportunities

Guaranteed speed of response

Named account executives

Professional speakers

Training advisers

Management consultants

3 Tactics and Strategies

4. Information

Sharing books on information

Press cuttings on items of mutual interest

5. Personal agendas

Hospitality

Corporate gifts

Introductions

Networking

Sales coaching

1:1 Coaching and mentoring

Ideas

Personal friendships

There are lots more. In your preparation stage, make sure you brainstorm all your options.

Relative value is a term used to describe perceived value. We all put different values on different things. Value is a perception. It is the seller's job to increase the perceived value and the buyer's job to reduce the perceived value. Here is an example of how a tea tray might have a different perceived value depending on where it is sold:

- In a department store it could be priced at £20

- In a big, expensive, branded London store such as Harrods, it might be priced at £100

- In a car boot sale it could be priced at £1 or less.

Same tray, same condition; different marketing and a different perceived value in the different locations.

Take five minutes to write down what your variables are:

Our Negotiable Variables

Variations on price:...

....

....

....

Other items:

....

....

....

....

....

....

Handling deadlock

You need to think the deadlock through and consider why you think things have stalled. This sometimes needs a little time and discussions with colleagues.

3
Tactics and Strategies

1. What are your first reactions?

Apply a mental icepack by bringing your emotions under check, it is natural to feel emotional at this stage, but it won't take you towards your goals and a successful outcome. Now isolate the reason for the deadlock.

Sort out your thoughts by ensuring your inner voice is positive. Look for common ground between both parties.

2. Evaluation

Summarise to give you a clear point from which to move on: what you have agreed, your respective initial positions and your original reasons for negotiating. Look for the positive in the other person's position and encourage them to look for the positive in your position. Work together to find a way forward, they have a stake in this as well as you. Look at the possible outcome if you don't reach agreement. Look at what might be underneath their refusal to move further, to find out why the negotiations are stalling.

3. Creative ways forward

Look at the bigger picture by using questions to find out the motivations behind the stated outcome and to help people think about the circumstances under which they might be prepared to move forward.

Take a fly on the wall approach to distance yourself from the situation in order to be able to see it more clearly.

Step into their shoes to see what the situation looks like from their side of the table.

Switch on your thinking by using the 'what if' approach, worst consequence approach.

What if ......this happens?

What is the worst thing that can happen?

What is the best thing that can happen?

What is the most likely thing to happen?

If all else fails, fall back on your alternative position and finish the negotiation there.

We often get our best ideas when we are waking up, just going to sleep, in the shower or in the car – the term is called alpha brain waves. When you do get these ideas, make sure you write them down as quickly as possible, as there is a tendency to quickly forget these inspirational thoughts.

3

Tactics and Strategies

Power Tips

- The magic words for trading concessions is, "If you do this for us – then we would be able to do that for you."

- You can always start high and come down, whereas it is very difficult to start low and go up.

- List your variables and the value to the other side.

14. Notes

14. Notes

15
How to Haggle

"The well skilled haggler has an 80% chance of bagging a bargain"

— Reshma Rumsey, TV reporter, ITV Meridian Survival Street

In the previous chapter we talked about bargaining now let's have a look at haggling. If you do not intend to have a long term relationship with the other side, then you will probably be haggling.

There is a fine line between bargaining and haggling, and some would say it's the same thing. However I would argue that bargaining is when we want a longer term relationship and haggling is a one off transaction.

Many people don't like haggling, but if you don't haggle then you are going to be paying more than perhaps you need to, most of the time.

I was asked on a radio interview recently, do I haggle for a "Big Mac". I think the interviewer was quite disappointed that I didn't. However whilst it is possible to haggle for most things, a Big Mac or a basket of groceries is probably just not worth it.

Remember everything and anything is negotiable but sometimes it might not be worth the effort, as the chances of success are small or non existent as in the case above.

Starbucks

Can you get a discount in Starbucks? This was a question I was asking myself, as I walked with 16 seminar participants out of Manchester University into a Starbucks. We had been evacuated due to a fire alarm being triggered.

I was working for Henley Management College and on the way out of the building, the course director, asked me if I wouldn't mind carrying on with the course in the coffee shop. "Yes "I said. Then she added "I expect you to get a discount as we are studying negotiation skills."

I had never heard of anybody getting a discount in Starbucks and I certainly hadn't tried. So I walked in, asked for 16 coffees and a 10% discount. The lady said yes.

As always in these situations I was wondering what would have happened if I had asked for 20%. However there is a fine line between pushing your luck, upsetting the other person and getting what you want.

If you don't ask – you don't give the other person
the chance to say Yes

When haggling you should use the same principles of any negotiation –

- Build rapport
- Ask nicely and listen

Television haggling

On the front page of my website **www.derekarden.com**, you can see a clip from a television programme I filmed with Meridian TV part of ITV here in the UK.

We made four haggling clips in Guildford market and there are some interesting points that came out. This is what happened:

Clip 1: Haggling for flowers. The flowers were priced at £3.25 a bunch. I asked if I could have a bunch for £2.50 and the flower seller offered two bunches for £5.50.

Of course this was 'Win Win'. I got a discount and the flower seller got an extra £2.25.

Clip 2: I was going to buy some CDs. They were £13 each, we haggled for two for £24, I then asked for five for £50. We settled at five for £60. I made the mistake of agreeing in haste, when I meant to say five for £55. I had agreed in a split second when I should have said no. The pressure of the TV cameras and the lights made me make the mistake. With hindsight I am sure I could have got five for £55.

This clip makes a very important point for haggling. Sometimes you just have to stop and think for a couple of seconds to review what has happened before you accept or make a counter offer. If you don't, you are likely to do what I did, say yes when there is potentially still a better deal to be had.

Take a few moments to consider the position before you agree.

Clip 3: I was looking to buy a picture frame. I asked the market stall holder how much it cost. He said £15. I said what about £10. He said "let me earn a living mate, tell you what I will do £12.50". I said what about a small frame thrown in as well. He agreed. I got

3

Tactics and Strategies

£2.50 off and small frame worth £2 to me and it probably only cost him 20p. The smaller frame was a negotiable variable. See chapter on bargaining.

Clip 4: In the final clip I went to buy a large house plant for £50. I offered £30, the lady said the best she could do was £40 and I walked away. The producer had asked me to show the viewers that sometimes you have to walk away.

Power Tips

- Remember be bold. Haggling isn't relationship negotiating. Always ask and ask again.

- Research prices on the internet and ask for the price to be matched.

- Don't get emotional about what you are buying. Buy if the price is right, don't buy it, if you don't want it just because the price is good. It's amazing how many things people have bought that they don't really want.

15. Notes

15. Notes

....
....
....
....
....
....
....
....
....
....
....
....
....
....
....
....
....
....
....
....

16
How to handle conflict

In any negotiation situation you will encounter conflict in differing degrees.

It can be really useful if you understand your conflict style.

Conflict is a fact of life. In negotiations you will often have conflict. Conflict can be damaging if not handled well.

In business, careers and life, disputes will arise with clients, customers, internally, with partners and friends.

Definition of conflict:

"Any situation where your concerns or desires differ from another person."

Your negotiation style is a critical variable when negotiating. This will be affected by conflict so the more you understand about yourself and others will help your success.

You will also react differently under different conditions and with different people.

One of the most popular psychological profiling instruments available is the Thomas-Kilmann Conflict Management Instrument (TKI). The TKI gives you the opportunity to understand your style and therefore start to understand the style of other people. This can help you minimise conflict and the damage to the relationship, helping you to work together.

The profiling tool was developed by two eminent psychologists in the 1970's. Kenneth W Thomas of the University of California, Los Angeles and Ralph H. Kilmann of the University of Pittsburgh. It only takes 10 minutes to complete and I have found the results remarkably accurate. I have used it with thousands of students, delegates and people I have been mentoring.

More than *6,000,000* copies of the TKI have been published since 1974. The TKI is also available in Spanish, French, Portuguese, Danish, Dutch, Swedish, and Chinese. The TKI is available from Oxford Psychological press in Oxford, United Kingdom both in paper or online.

No psychological instrument is perfect and it is important to hold a work or family conflict situation in your mind before you complete it. People tend to act marginally differently, in different circumstances.

There are noticeably some gender differences as well. Research at the Harvard Business School showed that generally women tend to behave more ethically than men and use fewer "dirty" negotiation tactics.

This Kilmann diagram shows where the five styles fit on a chart:

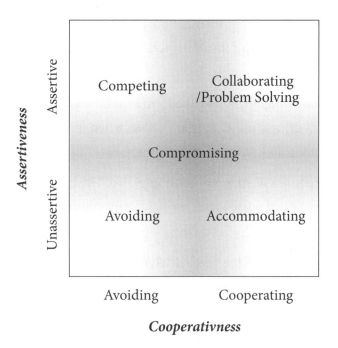

There are 5 conflict styles and one of these will be your preferred style.

By understanding that other people have different styles and recognising the style, you can adjust your style to help the situation.

Competing is assertive and uncooperative - an individual pursues his own concerns at the other person's expense.

This is a power oriented mode. Your ability to argue your own position, your rank or status in life and economic position.

Competing might mean 'standing up for your rights' defending a position which you believe is correct, or simply trying to win.

Accommodating is unassertive and cooperative - the opposite of competing.

When accommodating, an individual neglects his concerns to satisfy the concerns of the other person; there is an element of self-sacrifice in this mode.

Accommodating might take the form of selfless generosity or charity, obeying another person's orders when one would prefer not to, or yielding to another's point of view.

Avoiding is unassertive and uncooperative. The individual does not immediately pursue their own concerns or those of the other person.

They do not address the conflict. Avoiding might take the form of diplomatically side-stepping an issue, postponing an issue until a better time, or simply withdrawing from a threatening situation.

Collaborating is both assertive and co-operative - the opposite of avoiding.

Collaborating involves an attempt to work with the other person to find some solution which fully satisfies the concerns of both persons. It means digging into an issue to identify the underlying concerns of the two individuals and to find an alternative which meets both sets of concerns.

Collaborating between two persons might take the form of exploring a disagreement to learn from each other's insights. Colluding to resolve an issue which might have had them competing for resources, or confronting and trying to find a creative solution to an interpersonal problem.

Compromising is intermediate in both assertiveness and cooperativeness.

The objective is for some efficient, mutually acceptable solution which partially satisfies both parties. It falls in a middle ground between competing and accommodating.

Compromising gives up more than competing but less than accommodating. Likewise, it addresses an issue more directly than avoiding, but doesn't explore it in as much depth as collaborating.

Compromising might mean splitting the difference, exchanging concessions, or seeking a quick middle-ground position.

Working with a charity in Oxford, we quickly discovered that they had employed some remarkably hard working people who did a fantastic job raising donations and helping third world countries deal with all sorts of issues.

However we soon discovered that the majority of staff were "nice people" who avoided conflict and tended to trust people to give them the best price the first time. In reality this was not what happened. Some suppliers were taking advantage of their good nature.

We coached people to be a bit tougher, to move up the assertive scale when dealing with these issues and understand that it is necessary to be more assertive to achieve the charity's objectives.

If you haven't got time to obtain the questionnaire, I suggest you take a few minutes to think through your style. Consider the style of others that you know. Try changing your style a little to match theirs and see what happens.

3

Tactics and Strategies

No matter how thin you slice it,
there are always two sides to a disagreement

I recommend the use of Thomas-Kilmann profiling whenever you have a conflict situation, to enable a better understanding of the styles of the individuals. Higher self awareness means people will hopefully have a willingness to adapt their style for the circumstances.

Power Tips

- Understand your style.

- Adjust it to suit the circumstances and the other people.

- If you have a style which is dominant learn to moderate it to meet the circumstances.

16. Notes

16. Notes

17

The benefits of team negotiation

T.E.A.M.

Together Everybody Achieves More

Team Negotiations

Negotiating in teams is crucial to the success of your negotiating plans.

Any important negotiation needs more than one person involved. When you are directly involved in the negotiation bargaining process it is very difficult to concentrate on what you are doing and at the same time take notes, observe the body language and sense what is happening.

Depending on the importance of the deal you should choose the number and the roles of your team carefully. Briefing and de-briefing is very important.

What are the roles the team might adopt?

1. Lead Negotiator

The person who leads the discussions, controls the silences and calls the time outs.

2. Note taker

The responsibilities would also include back up to the leader if they need a break, writing the contract or writing the minutes from the meeting for approval.

3. Observer

The role is not passive. This person must watch everything carefully, the body language, the nuances, the tone and the feelings. The key time for input will be during the time outs, breaks and adjournments.

4. Expert

This can be the engineer, the technician, the product specialist or lawyer. Anyone you need there for their specialist knowledge. This person can be the most disruptive person to the objectives of the negotiation if not handled properly.

They need to be briefed very diligently as to when they can speak, as there is always a danger they might answer questions you pose to the other side. Sometimes this can be a natural thing to do for them, as they want to show off their knowledge to the other side.

They may have a close affinity to their opposite team member which can be used to your advantage or to your detriment.

5. Interpreter

There are some long negotiations where you will need more than one interpreter. The cultural issues need to be carefully understood and you might need separate advice. Make sure the interpreter understands your goals and is briefed on when the important issues require silence.

An interpreter interprets. They are more than a translator, who may be doing the job literally and merely converting the language. Make sure you use someone who understands the cultural nuances.

Seating Plans

Where do you and your team sit? Is it confrontation or cooperation you want? Sit opposite for confrontation. Break it up to be cooperative, across the side of the table.

Tough stuff, Police and Teams

I talked to the Assistant Chief Constable of Sussex Police who shared their strategy for hostage and dangerous negotiating situations. In the last 15 years negotiations have become more aggressive, with terrorist threats, increased psychological issues and drugs.

The police's role is to protect the public, minimise the threat to the safety of all those directly involved including hostages and hostage takers, as well as keep themselves safe. The role of the team in a police negotiation is similar to a business negotiation with a couple of exceptions:

1. The lead negotiator will not be the commander. The police set up a "cell" (team) to deal with the situation.

2. The commander, the decision maker, will not be involved in direct negotiation. Their role is to set the strategy and direction borne out of watching, observing, seeking other tactical advice with the objective of a peaceful resolution. They will site themselves away from "the cell" in the command centre. They make decisions on the tactical ploys and any other major decisions, sometimes without the negotiating cell's knowledge, if the situation dictates.

There is always a risk that the negotiator may give clues to the hostage takers, even in the most subtle body language, that something is about to happen.

The other roles in a hostage team are

- The speaker

- The listener

- The note-taker

- The firearms advisor (if appropriate).

Time can be very helpful as it can wear the other side down. Often tiredness can make people calm down.

Adam a lead negotiator of over 14 years police negotiating experience told me that recently he had been in a doctor's surgery for 7 hours with a person who had a Stanley knife.

On another occasion he had been on Beachy Head (a suicide hot spot on top of the cliffs close to Brighton) for 13 hours with someone who had found out his wife was cheating on him.

Fortunately in these two situations, thanks to his negotiation skills and the skills of the team, there was a positive outcome.

Rapport and Bore

Adam told me that patience, the ability to concentrate, resilience and perhaps being a bit boring helps. The more rapport the lead negotiator can build, usually the better the outcome.

The negotiator always uses higher authority when trading concessions. This is important and can be used very effectively in all negotiations. If the person asks for a cigarette, then the negotiator will ask the commander, who will in turn consider the tactical benefits of granting or not granting the request. In police negotiating terms this is called reciprocity: the responding to a positive action with a positive action or a negative action with a negative action.

They always trade concessions. They may want details about who is in the house, the position of different items, or they may not grant the request until the person leaves the house. They will promise fairness, they will promise to be as lenient as possible but they will not give anything that would compromise the situation. They work to a principle of telling the truth, and avoiding lies.

The team will set up an incident room (cell) so that they can write all the key issues round the room on charts so that nothing is missed.

We might forget what we are told, however we can remember it more easily if it is written up in front of us.

3 Tactics and Strategies

Other people who are listening may pick up additional information and interpret answers differently.

A director of a manufacturing company told me about a situation that had happened in Seoul, South Korea with the largest electronics company in that country.

His chief operating officer (COO) had gone there to negotiate a dispute on his own. He hired a translator who met him at the airport. The Koreans turned up with 17 people at the meeting, sitting in three lines, in order of seniority. The COO returned from Seoul and had a form of nervous breakdown he felt so stressed. He also believed that everything he said, the translator had passed on to the other side.

What can we learn from this story?

Always take someone with you to an important negotiation. Someone who is on your side, someone you can trust. Try to even the numbers up on your team with the other side, as long as it makes sense.

Realise in some countries, culture dictates that things will be different.

I subsequently learnt that in Korea everybody involved from administration, to manufacturing can ask to be involved in a collective decision on a big transaction.

You have to be resilient and able to stand back from the issues.

Power Tips

- Decide if you need to have the decision maker at the meeting.

- Set clear roles for the team, set your agenda. Learn from the police.

- Brief and debrief the team. Make sure the experts know what their roles are in the negotiation. They need to understand not to interrupt or answer questions that the team leader or the other side poses, without permission. They may be giving valuable information away.

17. Notes

Section 4:
Unlocking the Power

- Personal negotiations

- Key reminders for successful people

- Self-confidence

- Negotiation self-test

18
Personal negotiations

Practice, practice and practice

I have included this chapter for those of you who want some tips on how to handle your own situations. Treat personal negotiations as business negotiations and watch your skills improve. Keep practising.

Below are some of the 'soft' sentences and phrases you might use when you are negotiating discounts.

Caution: before using any of these phrases, remember the three golden rules:

1. Build rapport

2. Be friendly

3. Make sure they know you have options (drop it into the conversation)

When the price is mentioned, flinch.

The best kind of flinch is one that is visual, verbal and kinaesthetic (where the other person feels the emotion). So at that point go into acting mode and:

1. Take a deep breath, sigh out and scratch your head.

2. Pause and then say "Wow that was more than I was expecting to pay! Is there anything you can do to help me?"

3. Hold the silence - with a smile

Be ready for their reaction, but pretend you are surprised. This could go several ways.

1. You get a discount. If you do, ask for even more or ask for an extra thrown in, such as a battery or similar.

2. They say it is up to the manager. Ask to see the manager - and go through the same routine.

3. They say they can't help and you can either walk away or buy it.

Remember this is *fun* and not a game that you must win. There will be situations where nobody will get a discount. Don't fight battles you can't win. Don't take it personally, just move on.

Here are some more very powerful lines you could put into your own words

"That price is outside my budget! What can you do to help me?"

"If I pay that my partner / wife will go crazy."

"My boss expects me to get a discount - could you help me?"

"I am in a competition to see who can get the best discounts, you will help me won't you?"

"What flexibility do you have on price?" If they say none – say with a smile "I bet you have some?

"I need some flexibility on price. Is there something you can do to help me?"

Useful phrases when negotiating in shops:

"What discounts are you able to give?"

"If I buy this and this, what discount will you give me?"

"I would love to buy this but it is more than I have budgeted for. What can you do for me?"

"My wife / husband / partner will be very upset with me if I pay this much. However, I really do like it... Is there anything you can do to help me?"

"Can I have the usual discount please?"

Behavioural scientists explain that one of the reasons people are not good at negotiating for themselves is that they are emotionally involved in the problem.

Remember this when you are buying and try and keep yourself detached like you would in a business situation.

The more you can take your emotions out of the situation, the clearer your thoughts will be.

If you have to buy it today, you will display those signs both non-verbally and verbally. The seller will quickly realise no movement is necessary.

I was in the local branch of a well known chain of stationers and I was buying files and papers that added up to £48.74. I asked if I could have the "usual discount" as I do and the manager said "we only give discounts to students."

"That's OK" I said "because I am a mature student". He said "You will have to show me your student discount card". I said "I don't have one. However I study the highest achievers in the world and because I believe in life long learning and practice it, that makes me

4

Unlocking
the Power

183

a mature student." He said "That doesn't count. You have to show me the evidence." I replied that I could get a "mature student discount card" printed in an hour.

We were having a great laugh by this time and he then said "OK give me a break you can have your discount" and pressed the discount button on the till.

I walked up the road and went into my printers and saw Chris. I said "Chris, can you get me 1000 Mature Student Business Cards printed?"

An hour later I picked them up. I have attached one on the next page, please photocopy, write your name in and off you go.

Welcome to the Mature Students Club. After all you are reading this book which makes you a student of negotiation skills. Congratulations.

Also attached is the ultimate discount card. A piece of fun I am having with an American businessman and comedian, Tim Gard.

Power Tips

- Pick someone who looks friendly and build rapport.

- Make sure they know you have options.

- Ask them what they can do to help you on price. Then ask again. Always ask twice.

Your discount cards to cut-out and use:

19

Key reminders for successful people

"Most people know what to do and then don't do what they know".

— Jim Rohn

Do you do what you know?

Negotiation Aide Memoire

The term Aide Memoire has been used since 1846 to refer to notes, or memoranda, that are taken in order to jog one's memory later.

- **P**lan **P**repare and **P**ractice.

- **P**roper **P**reparation **P**revents **P**retty **P**oor **P**erformance.

- What is your **BP** - **TP** - **WAP** - **AP**

  Best position, Target position, Walk away position and Alternative position.

- What do you visualise their BP - TP - WAP - AP to be?

Have you checked your position to the real current market conditions?

What is the basis of your estimate of their real current position?

4

**Unlocking
the Power**

What are your 'negotiable variables?' – Extras / your relationship / hospitality / networking / friendships / leads / reciprocity etc.

How are you going to trade concessions?

- Start high?

- Start realistic to local market?

- Why do you think this will be best?

- What 'variables' will you use?

- Will you come down in small amounts?

- "If you - then we could / might……

Tactics

Does the customer price match, talk to other suppliers, have other accounts, play hardball.

What legitimate tactics might you use? Higher authority, good guy / bad guy, time limits?

Have you considered having someone else at the meeting, to help you read the body language and the signals?

Quality questions to break deadlock:

- How far are we apart?

- How close can you get to our price?

- What would I have to do to get this deal?

- What would I have to do to get a part of your business?

- Would that work for you?

- What are other people offering?

- What is the offer from the other side?

Could you let me have a copy of their offer for my committee / my people / my board?

Remember - People buy people - What's your secret?

Negotiation Debriefing – Aide Memoire

Always debrief a negotiation. Here is a another useful aide memoire for each negotiation.

What was the outcome of your negotiation? (In financial and ongoing relationship terms.)

Who made the first concession? What was it?

Were concessions given or traded?

How did people concede?

What tactics were used?

Did all parties have a BP – TP – WAP and AP?

What variables were used?

Did you use a time out? How effective was it?

Who controlled / dominated the meeting? How did they do that?

How did the other parties feel?

What body language did you see?

What was the most interesting thing that happened?

What would you do differently if you did this again?

Negotiation – Mentoring and Coaching aide memoire

The ability to mentor and coach the people who work with you and for you will help both your results and their results. Win Win.

Here is a reminder of the questions to ask the people you mentor and coach

Preparation

What do you want to achieve?

What will be the benefits of achieving this?

How much do you want to achieve it?

Write down how much you want it, on a scale of 1 -10.

What preparation have you done?

What else might you be able to do?

Afterwards

What went well?

What might you have done differently?

What surprises came up?

How did you handle them?

What concessions did you give?

How did you trade your concessions and what for?

What questions did you ask?

What was said?

What wasn't said?

What might you have asked with hindsight?

What might you have done with hindsight?

What will you do differently next time?

How are you going to follow up?

Is it a win win win?

What impression have you left?

What was your BP - TP - WAP - AP?

What tactics did you notice?

What tactics did you use?

How did they respond?

What body language did you notice?

How did you handle your body language?

Price and fee

Someone once said:

The more you charge - the more they believe

The more they believe - the more they take action

The more they take action - the better results they get

The better results they get - the happier they are to pay your fee

The less you charge - the less they believe

The less they believe - the less action they will take

The less action they take - the less results they will get

The less results they get - the more they will moan about your fee

Power Tips

- Photocopy these reminder sheets and diarise.

- Pass the tips and techniques around your colleagues and friends.

- Create a negotiating culture.

19. Notes

19. Notes

....

....

....

....

....

....

....

....

....

....

....

....

....

....

....

....

....

....

....

....

....

20
Self Confidence

Here is a chance to re-score your skills.

Now that you have nearly finished the book, re-score yourself on the Personal Assessment Scoresheet.

I am asked more about self confidence in negotiating than many other questions.

On the scoresheet confidence comes last. If you do not prepare and systematically check you have covered all the items before confidence, it will be difficult to be confident.

Over the page is another scoresheet for your convenience. Once you have filled it in, compare your score to the one at the front of the book. See how much you have improved. Decide how much further you can improve.

Just to remind you – here are the instructions again.

Recall a recent negotiation. Score yourself on your skills / ability in that negotiation and give yourself a score out of 5 where 5 = high and 1 = low.

4

**Unlocking
the Power**

Personal Assessment Scoresheet: Your negotiation IQ

(5 = high, 1 = low)

Preparation: .... x5 = ...

Questioning: .... x1 = ...

Listening Skills: .... x2 = ...

Interpreting Body Language: .... x1 = ...

Managing your own Body Language: .... x1 = ...

Empathy: .... x2 = ...

Understanding Negotiating Tactics: .... x2 = ...

Bargaining skills: .... x3 = ...

Inventing solutions: .... x2 = ...

Confidence: .... x1 = ...

Total: ....

If you want to improve your all round skills and negotiation results you need to work individually on these techniques, which directly affect the negotiation result.

Good all round negotiators should be scoring well over 80.

We can all improve and the difference that makes the difference to the success of your negotiations may be very small thing which may make a big difference.

Score again in three months time. At that time re-read the notes and consider how you can coach your key people to improve their skills.

Your confidence to negotiate should be much higher with your increased score. If you have realised how much you didn't know, then that is also good.

Negotiation takes practice. The more you practice the better you become and the more confident you become.

One of the biggest reasons for not feeling confident is lack of preparation.

If you do not feel confident, go back through this book, starting at the preparation chapter – Chapter 5 - Prepare, plan and perform.

Power Tips

- Use this as a reminder that we must always improve.

- Keep reviewing your negotiations.

- Negotiation takes practice.

4

Unlocking the Power

20. Notes

....
....
....
....
....
....
....
....
....
....
....
....
....
....
....
....
....
....
....
....

21
Negotiation self-test

Scenarios to look at and see how you get on

Here are a number of negotiation scenarios to test yourself.

Instructions:

1. Read the questions.

2. Then select the "most likely answer".

3. Then read the explanation.

Question 1

You have an urgent need for some legal advice, which you suspect could be expensive, on a contractual dispute with a client.

You have only an ad hoc arrangement with a lawyer whose services you have used but not for a while.

Are you most likely to:

- Write to or ring your lawyer, ask him for advice and then wait for his bill in due course?

- Write or ring and ask for a price before discussing the issue?

- Ring and negotiate the price beforehand?

4

Unlocking
the Power

Suggested answer

The first option is frequently chosen but has little to commend it. You have no control over the cost and it will be difficult, if not impossible, to begin negotiations once you have received the bill.

The second option has some merit in that you at least have a price and therefore some idea of the cost. However, if the price is based on an hourly rate and an estimate of how many hours will be required you still have no precise idea of the final outcome. It is worth considering under this option to ask for a fixed price (see Option 3 below) although it may not be forthcoming. If it is, but you feel it is too expensive at least you have a marker if you take your business elsewhere.

Option 3 allows you to negotiate a fixed price if possible but also allows you to negotiate an hourly rate and the maximum time to be charged, removing much of the uncertainty about the final bill. However, assessing what is reasonable would require you to check likely prices elsewhere which will also enable you to set your BP/TP/WAP framework.

Question 2

You have received an email from one of your best customers. They have expressed serious concern and disappointment on discovering that you are 20% more expensive than a competitor.

The customer feels particularly aggrieved because the relationship goes back 10 years and is wondering how much the relationship has been costing them.

Are you most likely to:

- Write back, justifying your service, delivery and cost base?

- Go and see them with key decision makers. Find out if they are comparing exactly the same products, how true the statement is and be prepared to make concessions if necessary?

- Ring them, listen and say it is impossible to compare one service with another?

Suggested answer

Option 1 is most likely to result in your losing the business without properly engaging with a very good customer, demonstrating some empathy with his position, and looking for a Win/Win/Win solution.

Option 3 is better in that you are giving the customer a chance to elaborate on his grievance but the suggested response, whilst it may be factually correct, will do nothing if the customer's perception is that he has been cheated. Perception is reality as far as an aggrieved customer is concerned.

The best option by far is Option 2. This has the best chance of preserving a valuable relationship. However remember even if you have to make concessions, and you probably will have to in these circumstances, always try to trade your concessions rather than just give them away.

Question 3

You turn up for a key negotiation and believe you are as well prepared as you can be. When you arrive at the client's premises you are surprised there are three people negotiating on their side including their corporate lawyer. You were expecting only to have to

4

Unlocking the Power

negotiate with the client.

Are you most likely to:

- Carry on regardless?

- Express your surprise, listen to their response then refer to your line manager for advice?

- Apologise that you neglected to check beforehand as part of your preparation what the structure was going to be and insist on a postponement and rescheduling?

Suggested answer

Option 1 is a possibility if you are brave, confident, and a very able negotiator. However, you must realize that you are immediately at a disadvantage in that the other team has the capacity to negotiate, listen, observe and take notes simultaneously and to use a variety of team negotiating tactics denied you because you are on your own. For instance, what do you do if the other team requests a time out to discuss or reconsider their position? Being on your own you would have no such facility.

Option 2 will not take you very far if you have constantly to refer to your line manager. Apart from anything else the other team knows straightaway that you do not have the requisite authority to agree to a deal and will probably gracefully decline to negotiate with you anyway.

Difficult though it appears at first sight, option 3 is the preferred option. Much better to suffer some minor embarrassment at this stage and live to fight on equal terms another day than to become involved in what may turn out to be a most unequal contest resulting in a Lose/Win outcome for you.

Question 4

You are at the end of protracted negotiations with a major supplier in Lyon, France. A deal has been struck at the eleventh hour. This is largely because the supplier is booked on the last plane back to Paris and her taxi is waiting to take her to the airport.

Whilst you would normally summarize everything that had been agreed, there wasn't time to do it.

Are you most likely to:

- Promise to send her an email.

- Ask her to send you an email.

- Suggest an exchange of emails.

- Wait for the contract to arrive.

Suggested answer

Whilst Option 3 sounds the most equitable it still leaves you open to the possibility of her sending you an email before you send yours and thereby seizing the high ground. For this reason it is not recommended and it follows therefore that neither are Options 2 or 4. In these circumstances described, you should assert that you will summarise matters in an email within a specified time. It is usually better to write the summary or minutes yourself anyway.

Question 5

In answering the previous question – you choose Option 1. Within minutes of sending your email you receive an email from her telling you that you have neglected to include the 2.5% discount that has been agreed. You can remember this being discussed but not that it was agreed.

Are you most likely to:

- Agree to it, because you are well above your walk away position?

- You email back saying you remember discussing it but it was not agreed?

- You "re-open" the negotiations?

Suggested answer

Don't agree unless either she provides evidence that it was agreed at the meeting or unless you obtain further concessions from her in exchange for the 2.5%.

Option 1 therefore is a non-starter. Option 2 is a possibility but could be the start of some serious confrontation as to who said what and who agreed to what. This is a perfect example of the need to take accurate notes and to summarise regularly through a negotiation. In this situation always calculate exactly what 2.5 % means in value to you and then make a business decision as to whether you can concede some or all of it; to keep the main deal in place and to strengthen the relationship with this supplier.

If you deal with this on a Win/Win/Win basis you are likely to benefit from some reciprocity from this supplier in the future. If you feel genuinely that you cannot just concede then you have to pursue Option 3 and re-open negotiations.

Question 6

You and a colleague/business partner are in the middle of a difficult negotiation with a customer. The stumbling block is price. The customer claims you are 10% more expensive than the leading supplier and, as a consequence, are looking to you to reduce your price by 12%, in return they will guarantee you volumes to more than compensate.

Are you most likely to:

- Agree but insist they sign the contract straight away?
- Call for a time out, so you can assess the situation and re-work the figures and come back with a counter offer to see their reaction?
- Walk away?

Suggested answer

Choosing to agree immediately as offered in Option 1 would be foolhardy in the extreme. You would be conceding a substantial element of your existing price for a promise, no more, of yet to be delivered or quantified increases in orders.

Furthermore, you would be doing this without checking the facts, the numbers or the consequences. For instance, if we assume that you are earning an average gross profit margin of 40% on sales to this customer and you agree the price reduction you will have to increase sales volumes by 43% just to stand still in sales value or revenue terms. Equally, walking away without doing the arithmetic does not make good business sense.

You should, therefore, take the opportunity offered by Option 2 to call for a time out to consider the numbers, the consequences, what concessions are tradeable, and the views of your colleague who has been watching and listening to the situation and therefore may have a different view to you. You can then discuss options, revise your BP / TP / WAP / AP and draft questions to ask when you go back in to drill down, discount spin and find out what their real WAP is with you.

Question 7

There has been a storm in your neighbourhood and several trees are down, slates have fallen from roofs and fences have been blown all over back gardens.

You have a number of slates off your roof and you are extremely worried about leaks and subsequent damage.

You notice a roofer already working on a roof across the road, and decide to ask him if he can give you a quote. He quotes £350 but says he is so busy he will not be available for three weeks

Are you more likely to:

- Contact your insurance company and make a claim? You have a £250 excess.

- Ask the roofer if he could do it now if you paid him £400 cash today?

- Ask him if he could come back as soon as possible and in the meantime get another quote?

Suggested answer

Your choice really depends upon how bad the roof is. With a £250 excess and a shortage of tradesmen, you might want to consider how much it is worth getting it done today. You might have to be prepared to go to say £450 to get the repairs done immediately. It might be worth it and your insurance company might pay out retrospectively anyway if you are a good customer.

Although you must also consider that most insurance policies have an emergency provision and will get you a repairer ASAP whom they will instruct. It depends on your insurance cover and the excess on your premium.

21. Notes

....
....
....
....
....
....
....
....
....
....
....
....
....
....
....
....
....
....
....
....
....

Glossary of negotiation terms

These are common terms used in negotiating. They are included because the simpler we can make the negotiating the easier it is to understand where the other party is coming from and then simpler to get a deal, Reading through these terms will give you ideas in your negotiations.

Active disciplined listening

An "active disciplined listener" is one who not only hears what the other party is saying, but also listens for the real meaning of what is being said.

Agenda

An agenda is a list of points to be discussed, which is introduced in advance of or at the outset of a negotiation meeting by one or both of the parties.

Aide Memoire

Literally "an aid to memory." (French) It is either a written summary of matters discussed or a prescribed checklist used to ensure nothing is missed.

Alternative position

A pre-determined position to which you will resort if you reach your Walk Away Position (WAP- see below) or negotiations fail. It represents what you will do with the resources that you have allocated to the transaction.

Aspirations

High goals (aspirations) in negotiations.

BATNA

This is an acronym for Best Alternative to a Negotiated Agreement. (see also 'Alternative Position').

Best Position

The most favourable position you wish to achieve as an outcome of a negotiation.

Body Language

The non-verbal language 'spoken' by the other party through their facial expressions, body posture and movements, gestures, and eye contact.

Bracketing

A tactic by which a speaker attempts to establish the other party's upper and lower boundaries.

Brainstorming

A creative process whereby people either individually or collectively bring out into the open all ideas, suggestions, and options for resolving issues.

Breach of Contract

A contractual breach is a failure to meet one or more of the terms of a legal agreement. Almost all except very simple contracts are breached in some way. Whilst only a 'material breach' is important to a negotiator they might fruitfully use "minor breaches" as trade-offs (see below).

Cards on the Table

As in 'Let's put our cards on the table!' It is an apparent request to establish an exchange of trust between parties and is an example of 'soft bargaining'.

Cherry Picking

A tactic whereby one side picks only those items it wants from among those in an almost settled deal.

Chinese Auction

Describes the tactic used by buyers whereby they claim they are also considering one or more other potential suppliers.

Comfort letter

A letter, which, although not legally binding, is offered by one side to the other to engender trust, where there is no legal contract. It depends on the relationship and what the party has to lose if it doesn't honour the letter.

Company Policy Tactic

As in, 'It is our company's policy that....' This is used as a tactic by some negotiators at the outset of negotiations to impose restrictions unfavourable to the other side.

Compromise Solution

In negotiation theory this identifies an agreement where neither party obtained all they wanted.

Conflict Management

Managing conflict by understanding the 5 different styles that people use. (See 'Thomas Kilmann').

Cost Analysis

This occurs where negotiators, seeking to uncover the seller's best price, start by trying to engage in an analysis of the seller's costs.

Cost Benefit Analysis

This is a process involving an analysis of the costs of a deal or project and then measuring these against the perceived benefits to assess whether it is worthwhile proceeding. It can also be used to compare one deal or project to another where a choice has to be made. When preparing for negotiation the analysis may be hypothetical as detailed actual costs and benefits may not be available.

Cost plus Contract

This is a particular type of contract, customary in some industries, such as food retailing, which can present difficulties. There is no total fixed price included but rather a demand that the costs incurred plus the addition of a percentage of the costs be the basis for the total contract price.

Cultivation - Gifts

The practice of successfully wooing a potential contractor by gifts is an ancient negotiation tactic. But today both legal (e.g. bribery, rebates) and ethical constraints make this less of an option.

However, there are other methods of very acceptable cultivation, including treating the other party with courtesy in a variety of ways. (See also 'Sweeteners')

Deadlock

This term describes a position where the negotiations have reached an impasse and neither party will move.

Deference

This refers to the deference or respectful giving way that one team member exhibits toward another during a negotiation session. The careful observer in team negotiations looks for subtle signs of deference to establish who is the boss on the other team, as this may not always be the lead negotiator.

Escalation

Conduct in which one party, having seemed in agreement, changes his or her mind and makes a higher demand on the other.

Experts

People in a team who have specialized knowledge and information, and are often referred to as subject experts.

Explanation of Failure

Helping the other party to explain to his or her boss why a negotiation failed can build goodwill and improve the potential for future business.

Face Saving

The process of reducing your's or somebody else's embarrassment, loss of pride or self-esteem, particularly in front of colleagues, line managers, or friends. Experienced negotiators anticipate providing a face saving opportunity for the other side.

Final Offer

A tactical thrust considered useful only after careful consideration, or where it reflects the truth.

First Offer

This is the initial suggestion as to price by one party or the other. In negotiation the first offer is rarely the final offer. It simply starts the process.

Flinch

An obvious body language or verbal reaction to a statement delivered by the other party. It can show disappointment, frustration, agreement, encouragement and a host of other emotions.

Folded Arms

A self-explanatory body position, which in body language terms can indicate more than one emotional reaction. It usually expresses a defensive position in negotiations.

Forward Movement

A description of a body movement, part of 'body language', which usually means that the party moving towards the other is in the process of attempting to agree.

Game Playing

Much bargaining behaviour looks like playing games, because of the use of moves and counter moves by the parties.

Goals

Setting negotiation goals or targets is vital to the process and success.

Good Guy/Bad Guy

The same as good cop/bad cop. This is where one person is approachable, sociable, friendly and understanding whereas the partner is aggressive, rude, and challenging. The good guy offers to help or to resolve issues in exchange for further information or concessions.

Haggling

Another expression given to an exchange of bids. Usually when it is just a one off transaction and not the start of a relationship

Hard Bargaining

Negotiation conduct in which a party consciously or unconsciously acts in an adversarial manner and in which trust in the other and openness are missing. (See also 'soft bargaining').

High Initial Demands

A bargaining tactic by which one party initially attempts to engender and diminish expectations on the other side.

Higher Authority

The claim by a negotiator that agreement on certain proposed terms would exceed his authority. It is a good way of sussing out the other side before it is put to the higher authority, which might be a committee, board or body.

Impossible Offers

The practice of making a proposition that one expects will be rejected out of hand.

Industry Pricing

In the preparation stage of negotiation, the discovery of patterns of industry pricing may identify the zone within which the price will likely be negotiated.

Lawyer Negotiators

Despite the reality that much conflict requires the services of lawyers, their role should be carefully considered.

Letter of Intent

A document that appears to set up a contract without actually doing so and is therefore not legally binding.

Linkage

The practice of tying one aspect of a proposal to another.

List Price

The price of a product or service as detailed on the latest list of prices published by the seller. Experienced negotiators treat 'list price' as a tactical ploy, hardly more than bargaining chatter irrelevant to the pending transaction.

Lowballing

An offer of an unexpected very favourable term in a negotiation. Such an offer is carefully evaluated by all but the naïve.

Lying

A lie is a statement made to another which, when properly interpreted by the recipient, is known by the speaker to be untrue.

Machiavellian

A negotiator who has confidence in his or her ability to influence others is said to possess the trait attributed by the Italian renaissance court observer Machiavelli to the Italian princes. His reputation for manipulating others is legendary.

Major Points

A bargaining session tends to deal with a number of points and it is common for parties to disguise their greater concerns.

Manoeuvre

The term 'manoeuvre' is a synonym for "tactic".

Mock Negotiations

Mock negotiation sessions are practice negotiation exercises through role playing.

Monetary Increment Game

The pattern in which concession behaviour is practiced. It is believed that the distance or spread between sequential offers or proposals affects the expectations and thus future behaviour of the other party.

Monkey on Your Back

Taking on other people's problems is equated to adopting the monkey on their back, an expression used by researchers at Harvard to describe the way in which people transfer their responsibilities to others.

Multiple Choice Questions

The practice of presenting multiple options, thus giving the other party a choice, avoids limiting them to 'Yes' or 'No' responses.

Negative Qualities

Recitation of negative qualities in the other party's product, service, or position is a tactic through which the user attempts to lower the expectations of the other party.

Negotiation Dance

A name given to the movement of changing positions between parties.

Negotiation Experts

Three groups have contributed to negotiation theory and practice; popular writers, academics, and seminar leaders and they form this group of experts.

Negotiation Goals

The advanced setting of negotiation goals is the preferred practice of experienced negotiators. These can be in different formats such as BP, TP, WAP, AP or BATNA for instance.

Nibbling

A tactic by which one party attempts to gain additional concessions, after the deal has seemingly been agreed.

Objective Criteria

Objective standards are being invoked when bargainers suggest that verifiable data be used in the session.

Open Price

A contractual term, by which the parties agree to set the price later, or allow the price to be set by the market. This is common in some businesses and in regard to certain products or services.

Opening Statements

An introductory speech, which may range from a simple pleasantry to the calculated employment of a tactic.

Opportunity Cost

The cost incurred or income lost by doing one thing whilst at the same time foregoing what you could have gained by doing something else, with the same resources.

Options

Choices available to the negotiator, which are fundamental to the negotiation process.

Patience

The ability to wait calmly and for long periods is one of the most valuable a negotiator can possess.

Perceived Power

This term describes the perception of the strength or authority that one party has of the other.

Personal Pleas

This is a tactic in which personal problems are incorporated into the negotiation, with a plea for help from the others. This behaviour, an emotional appeal, while commonly practiced, is ethically questionable.

Persuasive Personality

People who have or believe they have the ability to influence others tend to perform better than those lacking such belief and are described as being persuasive personalities.

Positional Bargaining

A hard-bargaining term identifying negotiation behaviour, which exhibits initial extreme positions on each side.

Power, perception of

Refers to the view one party holds of the power of the other party, whether it is real or imagined.

Precedent

Urging approval of terms based on past agreements, or on industry practice.

Preparation

The work undertaken in advance of a negotiation and perhaps the most important part of the process.

Price Increases

Announcing future possible price increases is a common tactic for softening up the customer.

Principled Negotiation

A negotiation theory that argues that there is an alternative to either hard or soft bargaining and that it can be related to a number of best practices.

Problem solving

Where both parties sit down to work out a win win situation together.

Put downs

The use of expressions to decrease expectations or otherwise persuade. There are varying degrees of aggressiveness both as to content and intent.

Quick Negotiations

This refers to quickly settled deals. These can produce extreme outcomes, which might leave a big winner and a big loser.

Quick Quote

Asking for a quick non-committal figure is a tactic used by the party requesting it.

Real Reason

The truth underneath the other party's position rather than the perceived or stated reason.

Restating Positions

Summarising where each party is in the negotiation thereby making the other party's position more explicit.

Restricted Authority

The claim by a negotiator that agreement on certain proposed terms would exceed his authority. Also called the 'higher authority tactic'.

Risk Taking

Successful negotiators are risk takers to different degrees.

Role Playing

A teaching technique used to practice negotiations.

Silence

Whilst self-explanatory it is important to note that silence is often used as a powerful tactic in negotiation. People used to say when there was deadlock the first one to speak loses.

Single Source

A negotiation mind-set causing the bargainers to believe that the supplier is unique in being able to supply particular products or services.

Situational Power

The perception that circumstances have placed a negotiator in a particularly favourable or difficult bargaining position.

Slips of the Tongue

Verbal slips occurring in a bargaining situation.

Small Talk

Conversation about rapport building issues, usually at the beginning of a bargaining session, 'to break the ice'.

Soft Bargaining

A negotiation approach, which purports to include trust, openness and cooperation between the parties.

It is sometimes called 'problem solving technique', 'I win, you win', 'partner's theory' or 'the equitable collaborative method.'

Speech Patterns

Include vocabulary, tone of expression, cadence and emphasis.

Split the Difference

Offering, after many proposals and counter proposals, a 50-50 split of the remaining difference.

Standard Form Or Clause

The word "standard" is frequently used in bargaining dialogue to indicate a usual position, which is non-negotiable or only negotiable exceptionally.

Sweetener

A concession offered to induce agreement or movement at the bargaining table.

Tactics

Tactical conduct employed to secure the objectives set by negotiation strategy.

Take it or Leave it

A risky technique intended to bring closure to a negotiation by issuance of an ultimatum.

Target Position

Where you would hope to end up.

Team Playing

Having more than one negotiator on a side. Roles must be carefully planned and rehearsed.

Telephone Negotiations

A risky form of negotiation as you cannot see the body language.

Thomas Kilmann conflict mode instrument

A psychology preference test to see which is your preferred conflict mode. By understanding this you can then adjust your style to be more like your perception of the other party.

Throwaways

A word describing items or terms one is willing to concede to the other side.

Time

Critical in negotiations and often used as a tactic as 80% of concessions are usually given in the last 20% of bargaining time.

Time Deadline

The practice of setting a time or date, by which, the other party must make a decision.

Time Out (sometimes called - adjournment, going to the balcony)

Taking a break to rethink, regroup and reconsider all options.

Timing

This is a reference to a negotiator's ability to determine at what moment to pursue a point or engage in a tactic.

Trade off preparation

In the planning stage each party classifies what terms are essential (a minus), what the company could live with (neutral) and what it could give away (a plus).

Trade Offs

The practice of making and receiving concessions.

Transference

See 'Monkey on your back.'

Type of Behaviour

Type A conduct: Persons are defined as aggressive or anxious. Type B conduct: The behaviour of a low-key negotiator, who in voice and mannerisms displays restraint in movement and language employed. Sometimes this is considered non-confrontational, yet it can hide a hard bargaining approach.

Umbrella Issues

When a negotiator has a hidden agenda this phrase describes the unexpressed "hidden under an umbrella" issues that make up the real agenda.

Venue

There is a school of thought holding that advantages accrue to a negotiator when the meeting is on his home ground.
It depends on his preparation. Sometimes a neutral venue can help co-operation.

Walk away position

The position where you would walk away from the negotiations. I recommend a soft walk away position in case the situation changes and you want to re-open the negotiations at a future stage.

Weak Position

The common fear that one's position is weaker than the other side's.

What if

A conjecture beginning with the question, 'What if....' designed to restart discussion by posing a possible concession or opening the other party to alternatives.

Yes Tag Questions

The practice of asking questions that suggest positive responses. The opposite is No tag questions which suggest a no answer.

Zero Defects

A negotiation ploy using this term to suggest very high product quality offerings.

ZOPA

Zone of potential agreement.

Recommended Reading

Getting to Yes — Fisher and Ury

Bargaining for Advantage — G Richard Shell

Getting Past No — William Ury

The Power of a Positive No — William Ury

Never Wrestle with a Pig — Mark McCormack

Everything is Negotiable — Gavin Kennedy

Influence Science and Practice — Robert Cialdini

How to be a Great Communicator — Nido Qubein

7 Habits of Highly Effective People — Steven Covey

The Ultimate Book on Body Language — Allan Pease

How to Win Friends and Influence People — Dale Carnegie

Use Your Head — Tony Buzan

Reading People — Jo-Ellen Dimitrius

Losing My Virginity — Sir Richard Branson

The Psychology of Persuasion — Robert Cialdini

Laws of Business Success — Brian Tracy

Think and Grow Rich — Napoleon Hill

Unlimited Power — Anthony Robbins

Man's Search for Meaning — Viktor Frankel

Men are from Mars — Women are from Venus – John Gray

Why Men don't Listen and Women can't Read Maps
— Allan and Barbara Pease

Acknowledgements

Thank you to all my friends, clients and colleagues who have helped me bring this idea of a win win book on negotiating to print. I apologise if I have missed anyone out.

Martin Kearns, Professor David Gray, Wendy Magill, Steve Pateman, Brian Rawle, Mike Ogilvie, Sir David Jones, Sir Gerry Robinson, Peter Hazell, Peter Hancock, David Knight, Barry Cole, Jim Ruffell, Will Kintish, Alison Brittain, Assistant Chief Constable Nick Wilkinson, Detective Superintendent Adam Hibbert, Michael Rendell, Matt Tumbridge, Peter Harvey, Jane Cranwell-Ward, Richard Bassett, Bernard Cowley, Godfrey Lancashire, Stephanie Watkins, Dan Poynter and many others

To Sally Arden for constantly proof reading the many draft copies. Mark Arden for the website and Jenny Arden for her advice.

Ayd Instone – for his ideas, design and practical advice.

I would like to recommend specifically:

The work of Dr Robert Cialdini which I have referred to in Chapter 13. He is one of the leading experts on the subject of influencing and more about his work can be found at www.influenceatwork.com together with some self tests.

The work of Thomas-Kilmann profiling tools which I have referred to in Chapter 16. These can be compiled on line with the results and feedback being received quickly and efficiently. The paper copies of the workbooks can be obtained from OPP, www.opp.eu.com.

Finally Professor David Gray, who is mentioned on the back cover, is Professor of Management Learning, University of Surrey, School of Management.

Notes

....
....
....
....
....
....
....
....
....
....
....
....
....
....
....
....
....
....
....
....
....
....

230

Derek's Inner Circle – Mentoring and Masterminding group

The Inner Circle Group (ICG) is a group of outstanding professionals. ICG members have access to Derek monthly to discuss issues, opportunities and any blockages to help them move forward. The cornerstone of membership are two unique events each year with Derek.

The events are designed as a think tank and a symposium. These are held in September and in February each year and they include input, discussions guest speakers and facilitation on leading edge ideas to maximise profits and personal gain. There is access to other member only events including private invitations to Derek's workshops, teleseminars and materials to enhance your business, your career and increase your income.

Derek will act as your personal mentor and advisor. You will receive a recommended book each quarter, and access to his development library with specific recommendations for your needs.

If you are serious about your business, career or personal goals and development this is a must.

A small group of ambitious executives are members of the Inner Circle. The circle meets twice a year, has monthly coaching and mentoring sessions, teleseminars and access to all leading material.

Derek's Monthly Executive Briefing

Monthly email briefing which goes out to 3500 plus subscribers on current topics with action packed learning and ideas. To subscribe go to the front page of www.derekarden.com

Derek's 1-1 Mentoring and Coaching

Often people like and benefit hugely from personal sessions to enhance their own skills without anyone else being involved.

Derek has mentored many people and helped them develop their skills.

Derek's clients include

PwC, Barclays, BarclaysCapital, Royal Bank of Scotland, NHS, LloydsTSB, IFS School of Finance, Henley Management College-University of Reading, Surrey University Business school, Association for Consultants and Engineers, Royal Haskoning, Oxfam, SEB Bank Sweden, Estonian Chamber of Commerce, Santander bank, Chartered Insurance Institute, Chartered Institute for Loss Adjusters, Buckinghamshire Community Services.

Derek has had many articles published including The Financial Times and The Daily Mail.